The Brain

*An Introduction to the Psychology of
the Human Brain and Behaviour*

Christine Temple

PENGUIN BOOKS

PENGUIN BOOKS

Published by the Penguin Group
Penguin Books Ltd, 27 Wrights Lane, London w8 5tz, England
Penguin Books USA Inc., 375 Hudson Street, New York, New York 10014, USA
Penguin Books Australia Ltd, Ringwood, Victoria, Australia
Penguin Books Canada Ltd, 10 Alcorn Avenue, Toronto, Ontario, Canada m4v 3b2
Penguin Books (NZ) Ltd, 182–190 Wairau Road, Auckland 10, New Zealand

Penguin Books Ltd, Registered Offices: Harmondsworth, Middlesex, England

First published 1993

10 9 8 7 6 5 4 3 2 1

Set in 10·5/13 pt Monophoto Ehrhardt
Typeset by Datix International Limited, Bungay, Suffolk
Printed in England by Clays Ltd, St Ives plc

To Diane Temple and Robert Temple who gave me nature and nurture.

Contents

Acknowledgements

The publishers are grateful to the following for their permission to reproduce illustration material. Although every effort has been made to contact copyright holders, we apologise to any that may have been omitted. For permission to reproduce figures not listed below, please apply to Penguin Books.

Figs 2.1 and 2.6: *Speech and Brain Mechanisms* by W. Penfield and L. Roberts, Princeton University Press, NJ.

Figs 2.2 and 2.12: *The Working Brain* by A.R. Luria, translated by Basil Haigh, Penguin Books 1973. Copyright Penguin Books Ltd 1973. Translation copyright Penguin Books Ltd 1973.

Fig. 2.4: Peter Cooper, Chartered Psychologist, London Phrenology Company.

Fig. 3.1: Vesalius's illustration of the position of the corpus callosum, courtesy of HarperCollins, New York.

Fig. 6.4: Examples from unusual views test (Warrington and Taylor, 1973). *Cortex*, *9*, 152–164, courtesy of Masson Italia Periodici S.r.1.

Fig 6.10: Examples of stimuli (De Haan, Young and Newcombe, 1987). *Cortex*, *23*, 312, courtesy of Masson Italia Periodici S.r.1. Also The Press Association. Permission arranged by Penguin.

Fig. 8.6: Courtesy of the Warren Museum, Harvard Medical School, Boston, Massachusetts.

Chapter One
Brain Cells and Brain Structure

Brain Cells

The rhyme says that little girls are made of sugar and spice and little boys are made of slugs and snails, but in reality the brains of little girls and little boys, slugs and snails, locusts and Nobel prize winners are made of **neurons**, the nerve cells which both form the basis for thought and control behaviour. All of these neurons contain sugar and spices. They metabolize carbohydrate from the bloodstream to give them the energy to function, and they emit and respond to **neurotransmitters** and **peptides** whose messages form the basis of the neuronal language of the brain.

Both the sugar and the spices are essential. If the level of carbohydrate in the blood supply drops too low, then you become hypoglycaemic and feel weak, dizzy and have difficulty in thinking straight. At the end of the London marathon, a few contestants may feel this way because their muscle cells have used up extra sugar, lowering the sugar level in the blood supply which also goes to the brain. The spices are also essential for thinking and behaviour. Imbalance or depletion of a neurotransmitter can create difficulty in the control of thinking and action. For example, in **Parkinson's disease**, we see the effects of depletion of the neurotransmitter **dopamine**. In this disease, pigmented cells in an area of the brain called the **substantia nigra** stop working properly and no longer release enough dopamine. There are effects on mood and thought, but the most conspicuous effects are difficulties in the initiation and control of movements.

Neurons also need oxygen to survive. This is brought to them, along with sugars and long-acting spices such as **hormones**, in the blood supply. If the blood supply to an area of the brain is disrupted – for example, if someone has a stroke – then the neurons in that area are deprived of oxygen and die. If the affected area of the brain had previously been involved in the control of movement, there may be residual paralysis; if it was an area that subserved language there may be residual speech and comprehension problems.

Neurons are very similar across species. Whilst slugs do not run marathons, get Parkinson's disease or develop language disorders, their neurons nevertheless metabolize carbohydrates, consume oxygen and communicate with each other using neurotransmitters. However, whereas a slug has a few hundred neurons, a human baby has 100,000,000,000 neurons linked into pathways.

Twenty years ago, textbooks were quite clear about how to describe neurons and these classical descriptions persist in many contemporary references. The original ideas were relatively simple but now we realize that the system is more sophisticated. The classical view of a neuron is given in fig. 1.1. The main **cell body** has spindly processes extending from it, referred to as **dendrites**, which receive stimulation from other neurons. The stimulation is either excitatory or inhibitory. If the balance of these excites the cell body sufficiently, the neuron's threshold of activation is reached and is triggered. This firing of the cell is said to be 'all or none'. So a neuron cannot fire strongly or weakly. If it wants to make an intense response, it has to fire more frequently.

The Traditional View

When the cell body is triggered, an action potential or spike passes down the axon of the neuron away from the cell body. This is a flow of electrical charge created by the inward and outward flow of ions across the membrane of the axon. The axon branches near its end. When the action potential reaches the ends of the branches it stimulates the **vesicles** of chemical neurotrans-

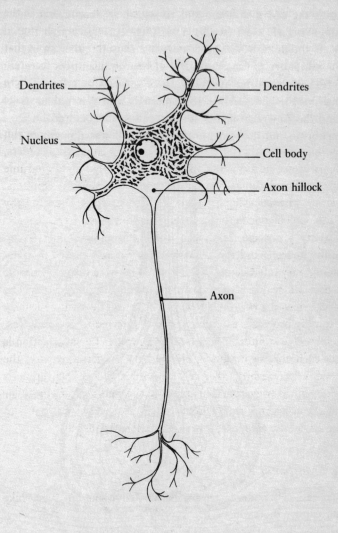

1.1 The classical view of a neuron.

mitter which are stored at the **axon terminals**. The vesicles fuse with the cell membrane and release their neurotransmitter into the **synaptic cleft** (see fig. 1.2). The neurotransmitter then contacts the dendrites of other neurons, causing either an excitatory or inhibitory effect. A handful of neurotransmitters were recognized: **dopamine**; **acetylcholine**; **serotonin**; **adrenalin**; **noradrenalin** and **GABA**. [Serotonin is also referred to as 5HT and the American names for adrenalin and noradrenalin are epinephrine and norepinephrine.] Each cell was thought to release

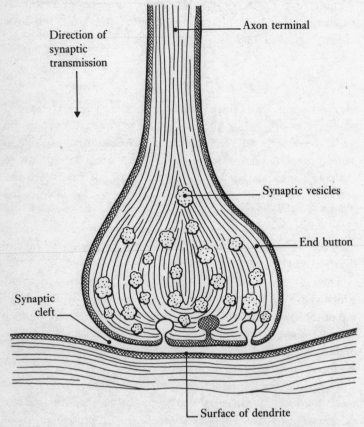

Direction of synaptic transmission

Axon terminal

Synaptic vesicles

End button

Synaptic cleft

Surface of dendrite

1.2 Synaptic transmission at the axon terminal.

only one neurotransmitter, the effects of which were always the same. GABA was an inhibitory neurotransmitter whereas dopamine was excitatory. Explanations of many psychiatric illnesses were postulated in relation to an excess or depletion of one or two of these neurotransmitters; **epilepsy** was discussed in relation to an overall excess of excitation or a depletion of inhibition.

The traditional view of synapses was that they were either **Type I** excitatory synapses, with an asymmetrical membrane thicker on the postsynaptic side, or **Type II** inhibitory synapses with symmetric membrane specializations. The synaptic cleft is smaller in Type II than Type I and there is a smaller zone of apposition.

Current Complications

We now know that things are not so simple. There are several modifications regarding the location of synapses. Dendrites do not always simply receive stimulation. Some dendrites are able to synapse directly on to other dendrites, so the directional flow of the communication can go both ways (see fig. 1.3b). When the cell body integrates the stimulation which is coming in from the dendrites, its procedure is affected by where the dendrite has been contacted. A synapse close to the cell body carries greater weight than a synapse further out on the periphery, or on the dendritic spines which cover the dendrites.

The output from the cell body may also be effected by axons which synapse, not on dendrites, but on the **axon hillock** at the top of the axon (see fig. 1.3c). Axons can also synapse on to other axon terminals where they can modulate the transmitter release of the axon terminal they contact (see fig. 1.3d). To further complicate things, some neurons do not have axons at all (see fig. 1.3e).

There has been a quiet revolution in the study of neurotransmitters caused by the discovery that many distinct peptides can act as neurotransmitters. Peptides are fragments of protein chains of **amino acids** and there are several hundred which can cause

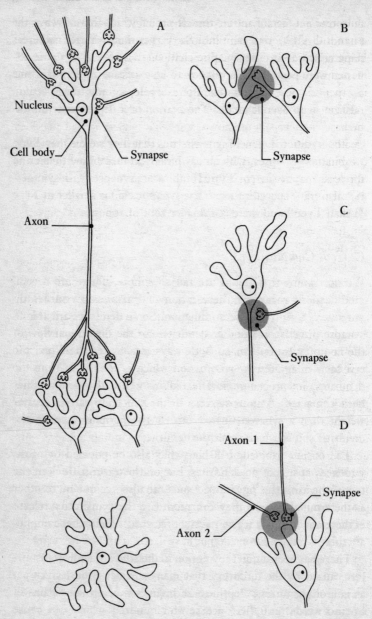

Nucleus

Cell body

Synapse

Axon

A

B

Synapse

C

Synapse

D

Axon 1

Synapse

Axon 2

neurotransmission. Each neuron is probably capable of releasing a handful of different peptides. So, rather than a single chemical being released into the synaptic cleft, there is release of a cocktail of neurotransmitters. Neurons may also release more than one non-peptide neurotransmitter. For example, serotonin may be co-localized with acetylcholine. The code carried by the interaction of these chemicals is unknown, but what is clear is that peptides greatly expand the signalling properties of neurons. The particular combination of neurotransmitters has significance but their ratio of release may also carry information. The influence of the cocktail will also be affected by the site of contact since the effect of a given transmitter depends upon the kind of receptor it contacts. So, for example, acetylcholine can be either excitatory or inhibitory depending upon where it acts.

Peptides do not simply modulate the activity of the traditional neurotransmitters. They may themselves have direct activational effects and may also stimulate a cascade of persistent events. Both traditional and peptide neurotransmitters can act at a distance. Noradrenalin and **insulin** are examples of non-peptide and peptide neurotransmitters which are also hormones and therefore can have long-lasting effects in the bloodstream.

In addition to the importance of amino acid chains within peptides for the communication systems of cells, these chains are also involved in the genetic code which determines how the brain develops. Within every cell of the body, including neurons, our genetic code is carried in **DNA** which is composed of protein sequences of amino acids. There is much contemporary interest in investigating the precise sequence of these acids. In relation to the brain, there is further interest in studying the protein sequences in families where members have a common behavioural

1.3 Variations from the classical view of neurons and synapses: (A) Traditional view; (B) A dendrite synapsing on to a dendrite; (C) A dendrite synapsing on to an axon hillock; (D) An axon synapsing on to another axon terminal; (E) A neuron with no axon.

pattern – for example, in the study of vulnerability to certain psychiatric illnesses. Compounds called **restriction enzymes** can home in on particular amino acid sequences, called **restriction sites**, and cut the protein chain creating fragments. Mutations in the codes of particular families may alter or eliminate the restriction site for certain enzymes thereby producing fragments with a different form and a different sequence of amino acids. These **restriction fragment length polymorphisms** (RFLPs) act as markers. Certain descendants in the family will carry the RFLP, so these common variations in the DNA sequence can be used to follow the inheritance of a region in families.

Having made a basic study of genetic codes within neurons we are now going to take a substantial leap up the scale and focus upon the structure and anatomy of the brain which is made up of millions of combined neurons. Readers who are less interested in structure and form and more interested in behavioural information may wish to skip this following section. However, the details are included here since a cursory knowledge of the neuroanatomy of the brain may be helpful in understanding elements of subsequent chapters.

Brain Structure and Neuroanatomy

It is easier to describe in words the activities and behaviours of people within the City of London than it is to describe the relative positions of the buildings in the streets, since the spatial geography of London is most easily grasped if you are looking at a map. Similarly, in descriptions of the brain and its activities, it is much easier to describe in words the behaviours and activities which the brain controls than to describe the relationship between its anatomical structures and parts. To get a clear impression of brain structure and neuroanatomy, it is best to study books which are replete with colour templates, photographs and illustrations of the pictorial beauty of the brain's anatomy. No biology textbook description of a flower does justice to the intricacy and delicacy of its structure, and neither do the cursory descriptions which will follow of the structure and neuroanatomy of the brain do credit to the subtlety, complexity and simplicity of its layout and design.

The brain is, of course, a three-dimensional structure; describing in words the relationships between its parts is easier for certain parts and structures than for others. The interrelationship of the numerous small structures towards the centre poses greater difficulties than in major subdivisions.

At the top of the spinal cord, within the skull, lies the **medulla oblongata**, which forms the lowest part of the **brain stem**. In general in the human body, the term medulla is used to describe the inner regions of organs, the Latin word *medulla* meaning pith or marrow. The medulla oblongata is, as its name also suggests, oblong-shaped and wider and thicker than the spinal cord. Above the medulla oblongata lies the **pons**; behind the medulla oblongata and the pons is the **cerebellum**. The pons is about two to three centimetres long and is named after its appearance, which resembles a bridge connecting the right and left cerebellar hemispheres. The interrelationship of the medulla oblongata, the pons and the cerebellum is illustrated in fig. 1.4.

The cerebellum, a bulbous structure composed of two hemispheres, can be divided into three portions with different functions. The **archicerebellum** is phylogenetically the oldest part of the cerebellum. It receives vestibular stimuli from the inner ear and helps to maintain balance and equilibrium. If you spin round in circles so that you have difficulty in balancing, the archicerebellum, confused by the signals it is receiving from the vestibular organ in the inner ear, is partly to blame. The **paleocerebellum** receives touch and pressure information from the muscles and tendons, and helps to maintain posture and to carry out voluntary movements. The **neocerebellum** co-ordinates and facilitates voluntary movement and makes sure that the direction

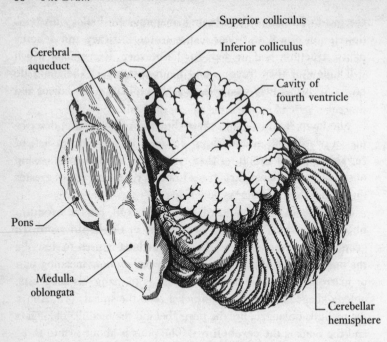

Superior colliculus

Inferior colliculus

Cerebral
aqueduct

Cavity of
fourth ventricle

Pons

Medulla
oblongata

Cerebellar
hemisphere

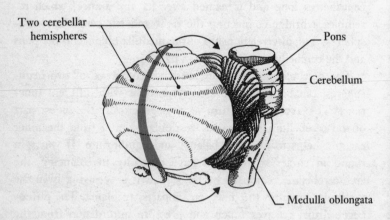

Two cerebellar
hemispheres

Pons

Cerebellum

Medulla oblongata

1.4 The brain stem/rhombencephalon.

and degree of the movement are correct, therefore, the neocerebellum is associated with fine voluntary movements whereas the paleocerebellum is more associated with the gross movements of the head and body. The cerebellum can be divided bilaterally into two distinct hemispheres, each having influence over the muscular activity on the same side of the body.

Within the brain are fluid-filled cavities called **ventricles** (see fig. 1.5). The lowest of these, the **fourth ventricle**, lies behind the pons and the medulla oblongata and in front of the cerebellum, has a tent-like shape and, like the other ventricles, is filled with **cerebrospinal fluid**. Hanging from the roof of the fourth ventricle is a network membrane formation called the **choroid plexus**. There are similar plexuses in the other ventricles, the **third ventricle** and the **lateral ventricles**, higher up the brain (see fig. 1.5). The cerebrospinal fluid circulating in the ventricular

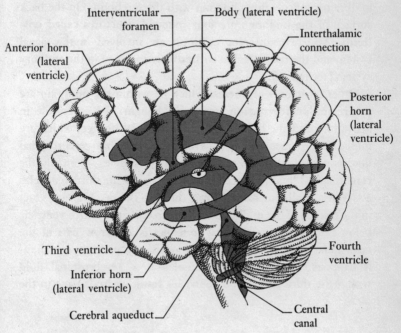

1.5 The ventricular system.

system is secreted from the plexuses. At the top of the fourth ventricle a canal called the **cerebral aqueduct** connects it to the rest of the ventricular system.

Underneath the floor of the fourth ventricle are several nuclei concerned with the maintenance of functions basic to life, which include the control of breathing, heartbeat, blood pressure and swallowing. The ventricles are very conspicuous on post-mortem of the brain, and for many centuries **Cell Doctrine** argued that the functions of the brain were distributed between the ventricles of the brain. We now know that it is the tissue surrounding the ventricles and covering the brain which is more critical.

The brain is conventionally divided into three different sections – working up from the spinal cord are the **rhombencephalon** or hindbrain (illustrated in fig. 1.4), then the **mesencephalon** or midbrain, and finally the **prosencephalon** or forebrain. The midbrain connects the hindbrain with the forebrain. On the back surface of the midbrain are four rounded structures called **colliculi**. The two **superior colliculi** are involved in the visual system and the two **inferior colliculi** are involved in the auditory system (see fig. 1.6).

Other structures of interest which lie within the midbrain are the **reticular formation**, which is thought to have a role in activation, and the base of the **mammillary bodies**, which are implicated in memory. We have mentioned that cerebrospinal fluid is generated in the plexuses of the ventricles. Normally the cerebrospinal fluid produced in the lateral and the third ventricles above the midbrain passes down through the cerebral aqueduct in the middle of the midbrain in order to enter the fourth ventricle below. However, the cerebral aqueduct is a narrow part of the ventricular system and may be blocked by pressure which, if it happens, can cause an accumulation of cerebrospinal fluid within the third and lateral ventricles resulting in damage to the

1.6 The midbrain/mesencephalon.

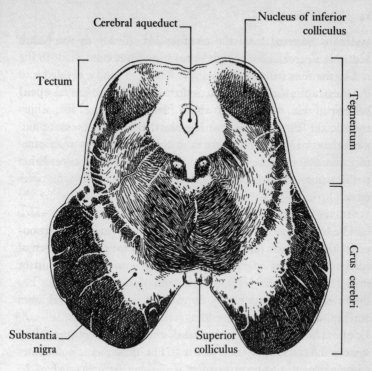

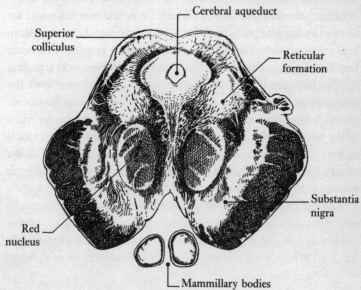

midbrain. Such an accumulation of fluid is called **hydrocephalus** and can cause enlargement of the head in childhood.

Moving forward and upward, the forebrain can be divided into the **diencephalon**, which makes up the centre, and the **cerebral hemispheres**, outside and above. In the middle of the diencephalon lies the third ventricle filled with cerebrospinal fluid. There are many small structures in the diencephalon with complex interconnections. On the under surface of the diencephalon is the **optic chiasm**, within which visual tracts from the eyes cross.

On the upper surface of the diencephalon there is a thick bundle of fibres called the **fornix**. The fornix connects the **hippocampus** which sits just inside the **temporal lobes** of the cerebral cortex and curves over the **thalamus** to meet the mammillary bodies. The fornix, hippocampus and mammillary bodies are critically involved in memory function, as are the temporal lobes which lie over the hippocampus.

The major part of the diencephalon, and situated on either side of the third ventricle, is the thalamus. The thalamus is sometimes called a relay station because it acts as a bridge between much of the information which goes in and out of the cerebral hemispheres. One of the swellings on the thalamus is called the **lateral geniculate body** which is involved with the visual system and lies on a route between the optic chiasm and the visual areas of the cerebral cortex.

The **hypothalamus** lies between the optic chiasm and the mammillary bodies and is involved in many regulatory functions. Tracts within or near the hypothalamus are involved in the regulation of eating, drinking, temperature control and mood. It used to be believed that the hypothalamus contained a feeding and a satiety centre which switched eating on and off but this has proved to be a simplification.

The two cerebral hemispheres lie outside and above the diencephalic structures and the convoluted external appearance of the **cortex** is striking if you look at the brain from the outside (see fig. 1.7). Whilst we share many diencephalic structures with lower

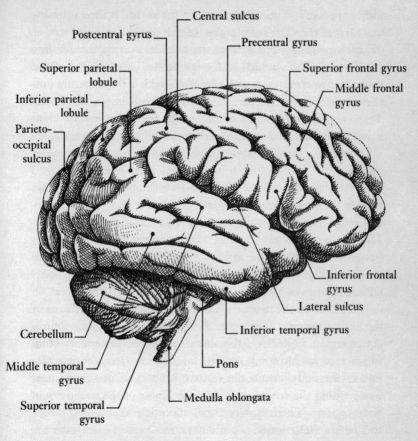

Central sulcus

Postcentral gyrus

Precentral gyrus

Superior parietal lobule

Superior frontal gyrus

Inferior parietal lobule

Middle frontal gyrus

Parieto-occipital sulcus

Inferior frontal gyrus

Lateral sulcus

Inferior temporal gyrus

Cerebellum

Middle temporal gyrus

Pons

Superior temporal gyrus

Medulla oblongata

1.7 The cerebral hemispheres.

animals, the cortex in man is substantially more elaborated than that of lower animals. The major element in this elaboration is an increase in size. However, not all three dimensions of the cortex have increased comparably. It has remained of approximately similar thickness but has increased sideways in both directions. So an area smaller than a facecloth in many species increases to the size of a family rug in man. As the surface area of the cortex has increased in size it has had to fold up on itself in order to fit within the skull. The surface area of the cortex is thus substantially larger than the surface area of the skull. The infoldings of the cortex, which appear from the outside as deep fissures, are called **sulci**. The outfolds or bumps on the outer surface of the cortex are referred to as **gyri**. In cross-section the structure and relative distribution of cells and different cell layers within the cortex remains relatively constant across species, including man, although in the visual cortex there is a doubling of cell density.

In order to facilitate description of the cerebral hemispheres they are divided into four **lobes** (see fig. 1.7). The division into lobes is made on the basis of two major sulci: the **central sulcus** and the **lateral sulcus**. The area in front of the central sulcus and above the lateral sulcus is referred to as the **frontal lobe**. The area immediately anterior to the central sulcus within the frontal lobe contains the **motor strip**. This region is involved with the initiation of movements of the opposite side of the body. Different areas of the body are represented in different areas on the motor strip; the proportion of tissue allocated to each area of the body represents the degree of sophistication in motor control of that region. Posterior to the central sulcus lies the **sensory strip** which receives incoming sensory information from the opposite side of the body. Again the relative proportion of allocation of tissue within the sensory strip is an indicator of the sensitivity of body regions. There is substantial allocation to the lips, mouth and hands, with lesser allocation to the back. If you take the volume of tissue allocated to each area of the body and construct a diagram of a person, which takes into account these proportions, you can produce what is called a **homunculus** or little man (see fig. 1.8). This homunculus illustrates the extensive cerebral connections there are to particular regions of the body.

The lateral sulcus initially runs at an approximately horizontal level but rises upwards as it proceeds further back in the brain (see fig. 1.7). The major protrusions or gyri within the frontal lobes are given different names – for example, the following are distinguished: **superior frontal gyrus, middle frontal gyrus**

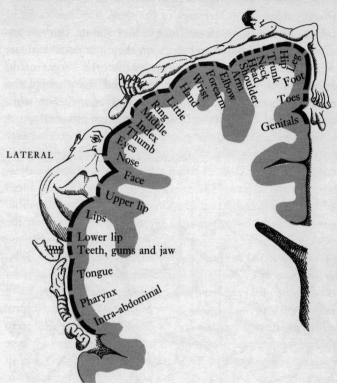

MEDIAL

Leg
Hip
Trunk
Neck
Head
Shoulder
Arm
Elbow
Forearm
Wrist
Hand
Little
Ring
Middle
Index
Thumb
Eyes
Nose
Face

Foot
Toes

Genitals

LATERAL

Upper lip
Lips
Lower lip
Teeth, gums and jaw
Tongue
Pharynx
Intra-abdominal

1.8 The homunculus of the sensory strip.

and **inferior frontal gyrus**. There are minor individual differences in the precise location of these gyri. Posterior to the central sulcus and above the lateral sulcus lies the **parietal lobe**. Below the lateral sulcus is the temporal lobe which is divided into three gyri by two sulci. The three gyri are the **superior temporal gyrus**, the **middle temporal gyrus** and the **inferior temporal gyrus**. The inferior temporal gyrus curves under the base of the brain and continues on to the interior lower surface of the hemisphere. At the back of the head lies the fourth lobe, the **occipital lobe**, which is concerned with visual function and is separated from the parietal lobe by a sulcus, referred to as the **parieto-occipital sulcus**.

If the brain is sectioned from front to back and the two cerebral hemispheres are separated (see fig. 1.9), then it is possible to see the structures which lie in the centre of the brain. Some of the structures which comprise the midbrain and the diencephalon have already been noted. Above these is a conspicuous white structure several centimetres in length, the **corpus callosum**,

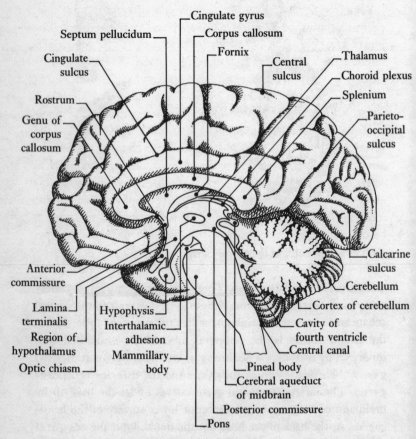

1.9 Internal view of the brain sectioned laterally.

which contains the millions of nerve fibres which connect one hemisphere of the brain to the other. The function of this structure and the difficulties which occur if the structure is either surgically sectioned or absent from birth are described in Chapter Three.

Inside the cerebral hemispheres lie the two lateral ventricles of the ventricular system, one within each hemisphere. So, within the ventricular system, the fourth ventricle rises along a midline axis through the cerebral aqueduct to the third ventricle. Then at the level of the lateral ventricles there is a division to each side, producing bilateral cavities filled with cerebrospinal fluid. The junction between the lateral ventricle and the third ventricle is referred to as the **interventricular foramen**. The lateral ventricles are curved in a semi-circle (see fig. 1.5). At the front end of the curve the ventricles extend into the frontal lobes; this area is referred to as the **anterior horn**. The lower end of the semi-circle extends into the temporal lobes and is referred to as the **inferior horn**. Approximately two-thirds of the way around the semi-circle is a posterior extension into the occipital lobe which is referred to as the **posterior horn**. Each lateral ventricle contains about 7–10 ml of cerebrospinal fluid. The fluid normally drains into the third ventricle through the interventricular foramen. A blockage of this foramen can also lead to hydrocephalus, in a similar fashion to blockage of the cerebral aqueduct.

Deeply placed within each cerebral hemisphere are a collection of nuclei, referred to as the **basal nuclei**. Amongst the basal nuclei is the **amygdala**, which forms one of the structures which are included within the limbic system and will be discussed in the last chapter of this book. The structures within the limbic system are thought to constitute a reverberating circuit which is involved in elements of emotion. Since the brain is a three-dimensional structure and the limbic system contains multiple structures, two-dimensional depictions are never very successful at illustrating the relative positions of the structures. Dominant structures within the limbic system include the hippocampus, the amygdala and the **anterior nucleus of the thalamus**. Major fibre tracts interconnecting these regions are also integrally involved. These include the fornix and the **mammillothalamic tract**.

The brain and spinal cord are surrounded by three different layers of membrane referred to as **meninges**. The most external of these is the **dura mater**, which is a strong and tough fibrous membrane. From the dura mater a number of protrusions extend into the cavity where the brain sits. The purpose of these protrusions, called **septa**, is to reduce the potential movement of the brain in rotation. The septa include the **falx cerebri** which is an extension of the dura mater that lies between and divides the two cerebral hemispheres.

The second meninges is the **arachnoid mater**, which is a more delicate membrane. Below the arachnoid mater is a fluid-filled cavity called the **subarachnoid space**, into which the cerebrospinal fluid, which is produced in the plexuses of the ventricles, drains through holes called foramina in the roof of the fourth ventricle. Finally, the fluid will enter the bloodstream through projections from the arachnoid called arachnoid villi. The cerebrospinal fluid removes the waste products generated during neuronal activity. Since the brain floats in the cerebrospinal fluid it also provides a cushion which helps the brain to be protected from minor injury. With more marked injuries, the brain will strike the walls of the skull or be affected by alteration in pressure or force which will cause structural damage. It is the susceptibility of the brain to this type of injury which has made sports, such as boxing, of concern. Also lying within the subarachnoid space are the four arteries of the brain which supply the blood needed for the survival of neurons.

Moving in from the dura mater and arachnoid mater is the innermost of the meninges, the **pia mater**. This membrane lies close to the surface of the cortex, covering the gyri and following them into the sulci. Cerebral arteries coming into the brain carry a sheath of pia mater around them.

Chapter Two
Localization of Function: Which Bits Do What

We learn in biology lessons that the liver detoxifies and the heart pumps blood around the body. Each of these organs has a specific function. When dealing with the sensory organs that feed information into the brain, we can also be quite specific. We use the eyes to bring in visual information, the ears for auditory information and the nose for olfactory information. Within the brain itself, which bits do what?

If I was having a conversation and somebody asked me which bit of the brain was making me speak, there would be some justification in pointing to an area on the left-hand side of my head towards the front and saying, 'Well, it is happening around here.' In selecting this area, I would not mean that the rest of my brain was completely inactive but that, in the majority of right handers, there is an area towards the front of the left-hand side of the brain which is involved with the production of language. It is the zone that lies around a region called **Broca's area**, first described by Broca (see fig. 2.1) at the end of the nineteenth century, in relation to neurological patients who had difficulty in speaking. The patients had sustained strokes which damaged the **third frontal convolution** of the left hemisphere. Their difficulty in speaking did not result from a peripheral difficulty in moving the lips and the tongue and articulating speech sounds, but a higher-level difficulty in generating and organizing the utterance. Thus, one of Broca's stroke patients only used a single word 'tan'. The pattern of language difficulty described by Broca, a century ago, is called **Broca's aphasia** and is also seen nowadays.

2.1 Pierre Broca (1824–80).

Many studies this century have been precisely concerned with the issue of finding out which bits of the brain do what and the extent to which one can *localize* a function in a particular area of the brain. There have been attempts to localize other components of language and other skills and abilities, ranging from memory and planning to more specific skills such as face recognition and undefinable qualities such as a 'sense of humour'.

A Little History

The idea that there might be variation between areas of the brain, in terms of their responsibilities, is not new. The earliest surviving written record, suggesting that thinking and control processes of any sort should be localized in the brain, is in the *Edwin Smith Surgical Papyrus*, which was found in Luxor in 1862 and which dates back to 3000–2500 BC. This papyrus has two parts: an early part describing patients with particular surgical wounds, including injuries to the brain; and a later part making comments about the use of terms in the manuscript, possibly to explain words and labels which have become obsolete. The localization of specific control processes in the brain is also documented by Hippocrates who warned against probing a wound in the brain, lest it should cause paralysis of the opposite side of the body. Here, he showed recognition that each side of the brain controls the opposite side of the body.

The knowledge from these early observations was either lost or forgotten and through medieval times a doctrine referred to as **cell theory** was dominant. This theory concentrated upon the ventricles of the brain and suggested that different functions are localized within these large fluid-filled cavities, rather than within the brain tissue of the cerebral cortex (see fig. 2.2). There was

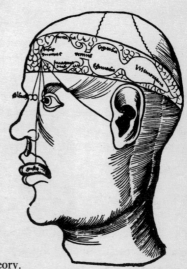

2.2 Medieval illustration of cell theory.

also much concern with finding the localization of the soul, which was variably located in different structures including both the **pineal gland** and the **corpus callosum**. Their central locations in the brain may have been critical in their selection.

Phrenology

At the turn of the nineteenth century, there was a renewed interest in the functions within the brain and the way in which they should be divided up and localized. Franz Josef Gall (see fig. 2.3) was working in Vienna, within a period when the city was a centre of creative thought. Gall believed that the different abilities of people were located in different areas of the brain and

2.3 Franz Josef Gall (1785–1828).

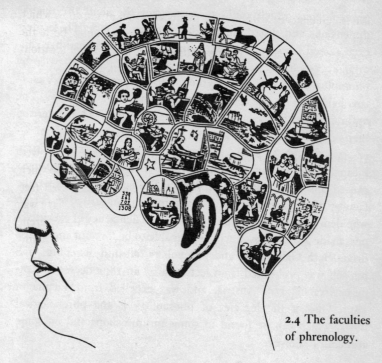

2.4 The faculties
of phrenology.

that these **faculties** were reflected in the size of the skull lying
over the areas associated with them (see fig. 2.4). Thus he believed
that, by measuring the size and dimensions of the skull, it was
possible to appraise the characteristics and personality of an individual. This belief in **phrenology** became widespread and the
ideas were brought to England by Gall's student, Spurzheim, on
a lecturing tour in 1814. For Gall (1810)

the development of the mind of the child, far from being a mere
moulding of it by the impression made upon it by its environment ...
is an unfolding of latent potentialities.

The Victorians took up these ideas with enthusiasm; in most
small towns there would be a phrenological surgery, where one
could go for the appropriate measurements by the sophisticated

phrenometers which could measure over the skull the relative dimensions and distribution of bumps (see fig 2.5). These ideas even gained royal respectability and Queen Victoria had her children's heads 'read'. George Eliot had her head shaved twice by phrenologists to facilitate the measurement process. The Victorians believed that one should strive for a balance of faculties. The optimum level of a faculty was an intermediate level, neither too high nor too low. For example, an excess of the faculty of *vivativeness* was thought to produce a hyperactive, over-tense disposition, incapable of relaxation, whereas a deficiency in vivativeness caused a soulless attitude or hollow feeling. An excess of the faculty of *executiveness* made an intolerant, destructive person who demands too much from people, but a deficiency of executiveness made a weak person who was unable to be forceful and lacked drive. Both Gall's ideas and phrenology fell into disrepute. Gall himself was prohibited from lecturing by an 1802 decree of Emperor Francis I of Austria, and was expelled from Vienna in 1817. One of the legacies of phrenology is the phrenological busts, which can be found in some antique shops and on some academics' shelves.

Cerebral Dominance

Gall located a centre for words and language in an anterior area of the brain; this localization was shown by Broca's study to be approximately correct for the production of language. However, after study of several of his patients, Broca concluded that it was the left side of the brain that was critical in this function. In the nineteenth century, Carl Wernicke also illustrated that the left-hand side of the brain was important in understanding language. He studied patients who had difficulty in understanding language and whose speech was fluent, but did not retain its appropriate sense. Together, these patients with difficulty in language comprehension had neurological damage which affected an area of the

2.5 A Victorian phrenometer.

brain in the left hemisphere, further back than the area described in Broca's studies. These studies provided the basis for the belief that the left-hand side of the brain was the dominant side of the brain because of its superiority in language processing.

The idea of a dominant or major hemisphere was held for some time. However, in more recent decades, John Hughlings Jackson (see fig. 2.6) pointed out that the right hemisphere of the brain was superior at certain skills, specifically in non-verbal spatial domains. Thus, whilst the left hemisphere appeared to be dominant for language, the right hemisphere was dominant for other functions. The idea of a major and minor hemisphere therefore receded but the idea of dominance was retained, linked to specific functions.

2.6 John
Hughlings Jackson
(1835–1911).

Mass Action

Not everybody agreed that it is possible to localize functions in this kind of way. Scientists, such as Head and Marie, argued that the language disorders seen in some patients were the result of general intellectual deterioration, and that they could not be divided into different types and sub-types which were then located in specific areas of the brain. If there is no differentiation in the brain, then the entire brain is involved in any thinking process. If the brain is damaged, the thinking processes will be disrupted but the severity of the disorder will simply depend upon the quantity of brain tissue which is damaged. This theory of **mass action** was supported by Lashley, who produced evidence to support his views from studies of rats running down mazes. In these experiments, rats were taught a route through a maze. Subsequently, a portion of their brain tissue was removed and, when they had recovered from the operation, they were retested on their memory for the maze route. Lashley claimed to demonstrate that more of the memory for the route was forgotten if large amounts of tissue were removed from the brain than if small amounts were removed, so that the impairment of the rat's memory depended on the volume of tissue removed. Replication of Lashley's studies has not tended to confirm this result.

These days it is fashionable to talk about the storage of information in **neural networks**, which are distributed across the brain. Similar to the ideas of the mass-action theorists, it is believed that these neural networks are disrupted if damaged, but the precise location of the damage may be less important than the number of neurons in the network which are destroyed. So, although general globalist accounts are not usually supported these days, there are echoes of their ideas in some contemporary work concerning memory storage in the brain.

Patients and Techniques

The rejection of globalist accounts of brain function was most clearly justified by the numerous studies of war veterans, who received gunshot wounds or shrapnel wounds in the world wars earlier this century. These patients displayed a variety of different disorders and the nature of their wounds often indicated that specific areas of the brain were affected. Many neurological diseases produce damage to focal areas of the brain, rather than the whole brain. Thus, patients who have brain tumours or strokes may have damage which affects a section of the brain. Other forms of brain damage, caused by infections or poisons, may have more generalized effects throughout the brain's tissue. These patients with brain damage provide information about the organization of the brain which would not otherwise be available.

Psychologists are sometimes asked if it is not exploitative to test these patients. However, many neurological patients who may have become more isolated from their friends and family because of their difficulties respond positively to the interest, attention and novelty of the investigator's test sessions, so there is often mutual benefit. In addition to studying individual patients, the contrast between patients also provides interesting information. Suppose we have two different patients: George has damage in area A of the brain and Edward has damage in area B. When we test George and Edward, we find that George has difficulty in recognizing faces, but no difficulty in recognizing another type of visually complex material, namely, written words. We test Edward and we see the reverse pattern. This patient has difficulty in recognizing written words, but no difficulty in recognizing faces. He can recognize people but cannot read. This pattern of difference between George and Edward is called a **double dissociation** which in this example could be used to support the idea that different areas of the brain are involved in recognizing faces and recognizing words.

In addition to neurological patients brain damaged as a result of injury or disease, there are other neurological patients whose condition necessitates surgical removal of tissue. These patients may have a **lobectomy**, where one section of the brain is cut, or, in extreme cases, a **hemispherectomy**, in which almost half of the brain is removed. These operations are sometimes carried out for the relief of intractable **epilepsy**, which has not responded in the normal way to conventional drugs. Epilepsy is a common neurological disorder and, in most cases, is relatively easily controlled by drugs. However, in some unfortunate cases the seizures are not controlled. The surgical procedures are rare operations of last resort, but provide new information about the localization of brain function.

Prior to some of these operations Penfield and Roberts (1959) conducted studies where they electrically stimulated the surface of the brain. In order to conduct the surgical operation a section of the skull was removed exposing the surface of the brain. The surgeon would be particularly interested in the location of language in order to minimize damage to these critical areas. Whilst the scalp contains pain receptors, the brain itself contains none, and there is no pain associated with stimulating the brain. Though the procedures of Penfield and Roberts sound somewhat gruesome, they were not painful to the patients. They would pass a very small current of electricity through a tiny electrode placed on the surface of the brain and ask the patients what they felt or experienced. The patients were fully conscious and, depending on which area of the brain was stimulated, might experience the sensation of hearing particular voices or of having difficulty with speech. With these studies, Penfield and Roberts mapped out areas on the surface of the brain which they thought reflected the areas of underlying tissue critically involved in the function which the patient reported. The areas involved in language are illustrated in fig. 2.7.

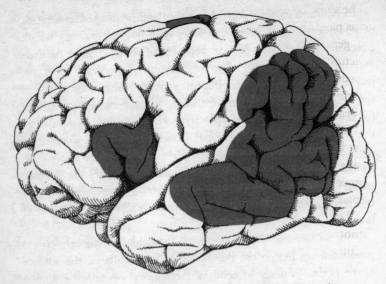

2.7 The language areas mapped by Penfield and Roberts (1959).

Brain Scans

Early quests to associate specific functions with specific areas of the brain were in part motivated by the desire to know the location of brain damage, when patients presented with particular symptoms. These interpretations are no longer so critical since the development of more sophisticated brain scanners in recent years. A sophisticated X-ray type of system referred to as **computerized tomography** or CT scanning, is in common usage in most hospitals. A more detailed picture emerges from **magnetic resonance imaging** (MRI). MRI is based on the principle that the different constituents of the brain are made up of component particles which rotate in different ways in a magnetic field, so that, for example, components with high water content respond differently to solid mass. In order to have the scan the patient must lie still for an extended period, within a very large magnet, from which the measurements and interpretations are derived.

The scan takes longer than a CT scan, and is also noisy, which is less pleasant for some of the patients. However, the picture which is generated at the end is very much more precise than the picture which emerges from the CT scan and enables more accurate anatomical localization in many cases. The greatest prohibition to the extensive use of MRI, both clinically and in research, is the high financial cost of the technique.

CT and MRI scans produce a static picture of structures in the brain. Our ability to localize function has also been substantially improved by the introduction of scans which look at active processing. These can either be based on blood flow, glucose uptake or the pattern of electrical activity generated by the brain.

The flow of blood in the brain is investigated using **single photon emission computed tomography**, so-called SPECT scans. It is now known that local blood flow varies with the functional and metabolical level of brain tissue. Studies of blood flow in different areas employ a radioactive isotope which is injected into the **carotid artery** leading into the brain or alternatively is inhaled in a non-invasive technique. The isotope attaches to red blood cells and the radioactivity counts from different brain regions are monitored. These counts can be transformed into *in vivo* measures of **regional cerebral blood flow**, rCBF. The effects may be highly localized and the spatial resolution of the commercially available systems is gradually improving in order to be able to make more precise interpretations from the information. Although blood flow has relatively good spatial resolution in terms of saying where something is happening, it requires the activity being recorded to be sustained for a period of time; thus it has rather poor temporal resolution.

When cells are active they use up glucose, which is circulating in the bloodstream. It is, therefore, possible to measure the metabolic rate of particular areas of the brain by looking at the amount of glucose they are consuming. This is done by attaching a radioactive label to the glucose and by detecting this on **positron emission tomography**, so-called PET scans. PET scans have shown that metabolic disturbances often extend far beyond the location of the primary damage, and are also more sensitive than CT scans. In the dementing disorders of old age, abnormalities on PET scans will show up much earlier than the signs of atrophy finally visible on CT scans.

When we think, the patterns of electrical activity over the surface of the brain alter. The overall pattern of electrical activity generated by the brain is referred to as an **electroencephalogram** or EEG (see fig. 2.8). Brief changes in the pattern of the electrical activity, which are generated in response to a specific

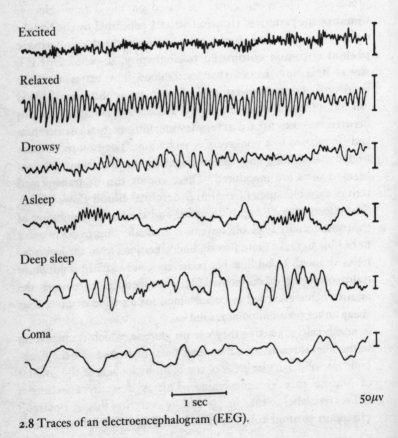

Excited

Relaxed

Drowsy

Asleep

Deep sleep

Coma

1 sec   50μv

2.8 Traces of an electroencephalogram (EEG).

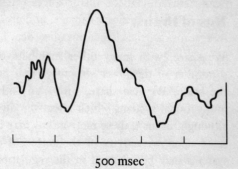

2.9 An evoked potential.   500 msec

stimulus, are referred to as **evoked potentials** or EPs (see fig. 2.9). For example, an evoked potential could reflect the change in electrical activity that might result from suddenly looking at a face or seeing a light flash. Both EEGs and EPs can be detected by attaching recording electrodes to the surface of the brain. This can be done by simply sticking the electrodes on to the scalp, in between the hair. It does not require any kind of surgical operation and is also painless. It is possible to record from multiple electrodes on different areas of the brain and, with computer assistance, to use this information to generate a picture of the electrical activity over the surface of the brain. The machines which do this are referred to as EEG **topographical mappers**. Critics argue that, whereas the spatial resolution of blood flow is fairly good but its temporal resolution is poor, the temporal resolution of EEG is good but its spatial resolution is poor. Thus, topographical maps can give a misleading impression of the specific spatial location. However, on the positive side, this technology is very cheap in comparison to other scanning technologies and, since it is non-invasive, it is possible to do studies of normal people as well as clinical subjects.

Bits of Brains

We share, with many other members of the animal kingdom, a number of the lower structures that lie beneath the cortex of the brain. We also share, with many other animals, some basic motivational systems which affect the direction of our behaviour although, in man, these motivations may be restrained and elaborated upon by activity in the cortex of the brain. Motivational systems may be involved in the regulation of hunger and eating behaviour, as well as thirst and drinking behaviour. They contribute to sexual desire and the repertoire of social activities associated with the pursuit of this goal; to a desire to maintain a steady body temperature, protecting us from cold and removing us from excessive heat. Further, they may contribute to the control of many of our emotional states and the modulation of anger and fear. I am going to illustrate the involvement of diencephalic and midbrain structures in motivational systems by discussing hunger, something which we share with other animals in the animal kingdom, but which in man is subject to sophisticated social and cultural influences.

Feeling Hungry: the Hypothalamus?

The control of hunger by structures in the hypothalamus was thought to be clearly understood over a decade ago. Subsequently we have found that what seemed a simple story is both inaccurate and insufficiently complex. The **hypothalamus** lies at the junction of the midbrain and the **thalamus** and consists of clusters of cells which each have their own nuclei. The hypothalamus and the thalamus lie within the **diencephalon** which is connected in front with the cerebral hemispheres and behind with the midbrain (see fig. 2.10). We know that the hypothalamus and the **pituitary** are strongly interconnected, have influence on other systems

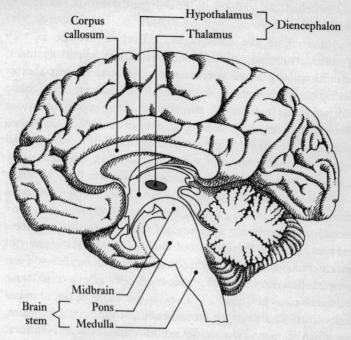

2.10 Section showing the thalamus and hypothalamus.

round them and release hormones which act on different glands in the body. The body has two types of glands: **exocrine glands**, which secrete on to the surface of the body, for example, sweat and tears; and **endocrine glands**, which secrete into the body cavities, as in the digestive system. They also act on glands which secrete hormones directly into the bloodstream. The hypothalamus acts upon endocrine rather than exocrine glands and is sometimes seen as linking reflexes of the body and the higher brain systems which mediate the expression of the motivations of hunger and thirst.

The early inaccurate hypothesis of the hypothalamus in relation to hunger suggested that it had a dual centre. The **ventromedial hypothalamus** was considered to be the area in which hunger was switched off, and the **lateral hypothalamus** the area in which hunger was switched on. These functional centres were hypothesized on the basis of the effects of damage to each of these structures. When the ventromedial hypothalamus is lesioned, an animal will overeat and continue to eat to a chronic elevated level. In humans, a similar effect has been described in patients with tumours of the ventromedial hypothalamus, in which excessively large numbers of calories can be consumed each day. In contrast, if the lateral hypothalamus is damaged, an animal will stop eating and will, if it eats at all, eat only a tiny amount of food, leading to substantial reduction in body weight.

The animal with ventromedial hypothalamic damage who has a tendency to overeat does not, however, respond to food in a normal way. It will not work as hard for food if it has to press a lever to get food. Schachter and Rodin (1974) investigated this feature in obese humans. Obese subjects and normal subjects were asked to carry out dull arithmetical sums in a room in which there was a bowl of nuts. For some of the subjects, the nuts had shells which had to be removed before the nuts could be eaten. For other subjects, the nuts did not have the shells and could be eaten instantly. The obese subjects ate large numbers of nuts if they did not have to remove their shells, but only small quantities of nuts if they had to remove the shells. The results were interpreted as indicating that obese people were like the very hungry rats with ventromedial hypothalamic lesions and did not like to work hard for food. Ventromedial hypothalamic rats are also particularly sensitive to bad tasting food. If food is adulterated with an unpleasant taste, they will prefer not to eat it. Thus, they are rather finicky eaters, and Schachter and Rodin (1974) also produced evidence that obese people are finicky eaters.

The ventromedial animals do not continue to eat and become fatter and fatter and fatter. Their weight stabilizes at an elevated level and they can keep it constant at this elevated level. It is as if the set point on some type of homeostatic device has been raised, so that it is being switched off too late. The capacity to switch off eating has not been destroyed altogether.

If the **vagus nerve** which feeds into the ventromedial hypothalamus is cut, then ventromedial lesions do not lead to obesity. The vagus has both motor control nerves and sensory nerves from the stomach and intestinal tract and also to the heart and other organs. In some way the ventromedial lesion may alter the actions of the vagus nerve so that more eating occurs. If the stomach feels hungry, or if we experience hunger contractions, a person will eat more. It may be that sectioning the vagus nerve eliminates this appropriate feeling of hunger.

Animals who have had the lateral hypothalamus lesioned and are eating very little will also regulate their weight. If, for example, they are starved prior to their operations, so that at the time of operation their weight level is already greatly reduced, then when they recover they regulate their weight, even if that requires them to eat more and increase their weight from their chronically lowered level. Their final weight level is lower than it should be but it is monitored.

There are many other accompanying symptoms to lateral hypothalamic lesions. These include the neglect of other sensory stimuli. Lesioning of the lateral hypothalamus destroys the ascending pathways which carry dopamine in the brain. If a lesion is made only on one side of the lateral hypothalamus, the animal will ignore all the stimuli that are presented to it on that side. If the lesion is made on both sides, then its lack of responsiveness is more extensive. Therefore, the lack of response to food may be indicative of a general lack of responsiveness or inability to interpret and process appropriately the sensory stimuli which are input. Damage to dopaminergic tracts outside the lateral hypothalamus can induce a similar syndrome to that seen with lateral hypothalamic damage, so, the old dual-centre theory for the hypothalamus has proved too simplistic.

Animals must decide not only when to eat but what to eat.

Rolls and Rolls (1982) have conducted **single cell recording** from microelectrodes placed in cells in the hypothalamus and note that in some animals there are cells which fire in response to specific foods, but do not respond to other foods. Some of these cells are sensitive to the *taste* of the food, whilst other cells are responsive to the *sight* of the food. Rolls and Rolls claim that at the hypothalamic stage of processing, these visual and gustatory responses to food-related inputs are modulated by hunger. Hypothalamic neurons could mediate the responses which occur in the hungry animal to food, including both autonomic and endocrine responses, as well as feeding responses.

Identifying Edibles: the Amygdala?

In addition to selecting specific foods, animals must also learn to avoid specific foods. Rats are capable of very rapid learning in response to a single episode of poisoning. They exhibit **neophobia** when tackling a new food substance, so that they sample it in very tiny quantities which enables them to survive if the food is poisoned. If they become ill subsequent to eating, several hours later, then they will avoid the food substance which was taken prior to the sickness and thereby survive. This very rapid learning went against many of the early learning theorists' views of how animals learn. Standard **operant** and **classical conditioning** theories of learning required that for a stimulus and response to become associated they must be simultaneous or contiguous and that there must be repeated exposures. However, in rat poison avoidance, the sickness may be separated from the episode of food consumption by several hours and learning is rapid enough to occur after one episode.

Human subjects may also learn to avoid unpleasant-tasting substances in a similar way. Children who receive chemotherapy for leukaemia often feel sick. Bernstein (1978) conducted an experiment in which children were given the choice of different types of ice-cream to eat, a few hours before their treatment. The results showed that the children developed a rapid dislike to a distinctive-tasting new ice-cream when it was introduced in this way. Even when they knew that the ice-cream had not been responsible for the sickness, they still found that they had no desire to taste it again. Some of the fads and avoidances of pregnancy may also be linked to associations with the nausea that can be felt at that time.

Rapid learning to avoid a substance which produces illness would be very useful in both rats and man in enabling them to adapt to new geographical environments and modulate their food intake appropriately. A specific brain region has been proposed as the site of this ability. If the **amygdala** is destroyed, animals are unable to learn in this kind of way. Destruction of the amygdala seems to impair the capacity to make the appropriate judgements of what is a novel and what is not a novel food. There is both loss of the neophobia which reduces the volume of new foods which are tasted and failure to develop strong aversions to food stuffs which generate illness. The amygdala may also be important in other areas requiring the discrimination of stimuli to which particular responses are appropriate.

Cultural Complexities

In humans the selection of food is more complicated. There are certain substances for which we may feel an instinctive and innate dislike. For example, beer has a bitter taste, and the first sip of it taken by almost any human will seem unpleasant. Yet there is often strong cultural pressure to overcome this innate dislike. Having taken beer over a period of time it becomes apparent that there is no longer an instinctive revulsion to the liquid, indeed, the opposite may be true. Here, socially mediated exposure to a particular food stuff may lead to the internalization of a preference for it.

A similar case can be made for chilli pepper and has been

discussed by Rozin (1982). There is an innate aversion to chilli pepper, which is an irritant. However, there may be certain nutritional or pharmacological advantages associated with chilli; it may also have some role in emotional homeostasis since it is a stimulant. Gradually, chilli pepper was incorporated into the culture, becoming a flavour principal in cuisine. Exposure to chilli, as a flavour principal, is now widespread in Western cultures and people will seek out this flavour from preference, despite their initial distaste.

Innate sweet preferences can also be used to modulate food selection and sweeteners will increase our affection for and affinity to particular food stuffs. In these cases, cultural influences interact with the effects upon the brain of these food stuffs.

Further cultural taboos or recommendations may affect what we consume. For religious reasons people may avoid particular types of meat, and for social reasons people may avoid eating large quantities of cream cakes and other unhealthy substances which are incompatible with the healthy mode of our current culture. These health-related social pressures may also induce people to eat large quantities of apparently unappetizing beans, pulses and lettuces in order to satisfy their own ethical and moral perspectives on dietary consumption, as well as being concerned about the effect of the substances upon our bodies. In humans, food selection involves many ritualistic aspects, forming a part of social encounters and also major ceremonies marking changes in life. In these processes it is clear that higher cortical mechanisms are also involved.

Seeing Cream Cakes: the Occipital Lobes

The two cerebral hemispheres are divided into four different lobes (see fig. 2.11). The **occipital lobes** are involved in the processes connected with vision. Thus, when we walk past a cake shop or we scan the buffet table inspecting the food on offer, the

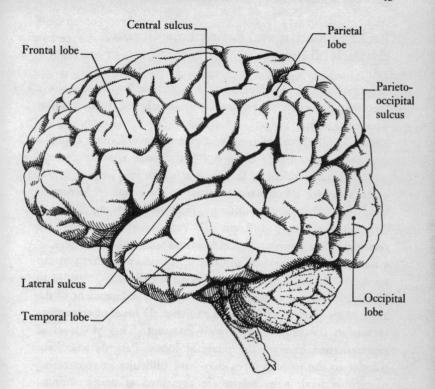

Central sulcus

Frontal lobe

Parietal lobe

Parieto-occipital sulcus

Lateral sulcus

Temporal lobe

Occipital lobe

2.11 The four lobes of the cerebral cortex.

sensory information relating to the different patterns of light intensity and colours produced by these visual arrays enters the eye, passes up the optic nerve and initially arrives in the cortex at the very base of the occipital lobe, at the back of the head. This visual information is then further refined, assimilated and analysed as it passes forward through the occipital lobe. Initially, the brain appears to process simply the lines, edges and discontinuities created by this array of sandwiches, cakes and other appetizing delicacies. Marr (1980) called the brain's initial representation of this information the **primal sketch**.

Peeling Bananas and Eating Your Greens: the Parietal Lobes

Marr's primal sketch feeds into a system in which there is a representation of the object itself which is affected by the angle at which the object is seen. It is said to be view-specific and is called the $2\frac{1}{2}$D level of representation. If you look at a quail's egg, caviar or a baked bean, it has the same approximate appearance, independent of the angle at which it is inspected, but other items are affected by the angle of inspection. A lobster or a banana will look very different from different angles. These different views have different $2\frac{1}{2}$D representations. If you are required to eat a lobster or peel a banana with a knife and fork, at a formal college ceremony in Oxford, it is essential that you can recognize the food item from different viewpoints. In order to have an integrated system to recognize items independent of the angle of viewing, Marr proposed a further **3D level of representation** in the brain that is view-invariant. This 3D level of representation involves the **parietal lobes**. Patients who have damage to the parietal lobes may have difficulty in recognizing objects or food items which are presented at unconventional angles. Further discussion of visual perception is found in Chapter Six.

In order to discuss further issues of localization it is necessary to describe a series of areas of the brain and their associated functions. These ideas will be introduced by discussing the course of a somewhat idealized evening out.

The parietal lobes are not just concerned with visual perception. They are also concerned with general **spatial orientation**. If you are driving to a restaurant, using a map to assist you, your parietal lobes will contribute to your navigational skill along the map route. They are involved in route-finding ability, making judgements about the relative positions of things on the map you are studying. Once you have parked your car and you are walking to the restaurant itself, the parietal lobes may also be involved in tracing the route and path to find the restaurant. Some people's parietal lobes seem to work better than others in this regard and there is conspicuous individual variation in the capacity to negotiate an unfamiliar place. When you get close to the restaurant, systems within your parietal lobes may recognize the front of the restaurant building.

Some of the reading abilities involved in inspecting the menu will arise from activities at the junctions between the occipital, parietal and **temporal lobes**, in the area referred to as the **angular gyrus**. As you sit in the restaurant, inspecting the menu and deciding what you wish to eat, you may feel that the chair on which you sit is uncomfortable or be aware of a draught on your legs. This perception of tactile stimuli is dominantly controlled by the parietal lobes. Further, your sensation of the position of your feet, crucial for certain flirtatious behaviours which may take place in the restaurant, is also dependent upon the parietal lobes. Your understanding of **body schema** and position – where your arms are; where your legs are; the tilt of your body; and the angle of your head – are all related to the activities of the parietal lobes. Awareness of these will be important if you are in a country like Switzerland or France, in which cultural manners suggest that the hands are kept above the table during dinner.

When your plate of food finally arrives you will focus your attention upon it and systematically eat your way through the meal, assuming it is living up to expectation. In controlling and directing your attention over this plate of food the parietal lobes are further involved. Following damage to the parietal lobes, some neurological patients display a syndrome referred to as **neglect**, in which they will ignore certain aspects on one side of the world in front of them (see fig. 2.12). In some cases of neglect, when a patient tries to eat a plate of food, they may ignore some of the food lying on one side. Typically, it is the right-hand side of the plate of food which would be ignored, rather than the left. In some cases, up to half of the food could

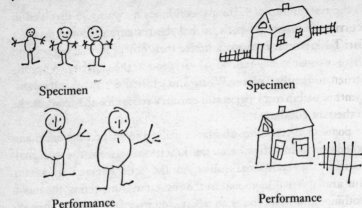

Specimen   Specimen

Performance   Performance

2.12 Copying by a patient with neglect (after Luria, 1973).

be left, going almost up to the mid-line of the plate of food. If someone with neglect failed to eat the food on the right of their plate, then if the plate was turned around completely, so that the food which had been on the right-hand side of the plate, now lay on the left-hand side, the neglected food might be noticed. Ignoring the right-hand side of the plate may result from the disruption of the attentional control mechanisms in the parietal lobes, which are dominantly controlled in the right cerebral hemisphere.

In dissecting your fish or fowl, you may be faced with a rather complex series of actions, requiring you to hold parts still on your plate, whilst you tackle the removal of the portions you wish to eat. Vegetarian meals can also require a complex sequencing of motor movements in the balancing of large amounts of beans, pulses and vegetables on your knife and fork. These activities of cutting, sequencing and organizing movements are disrupted in some cases of **constructional apraxia**. Here, it is not possible to organize a sequence of co-ordinated movements in order to attain a goal and the parietal lobes have also been implicated in this disorder.

Remembering Jokes and Eavesdropping: the Temporal Lobes

Structures in the **inferior temporal lobes** are involved in elements of object recognition and also face recognition. With damage to these regions and those bordering the parietal lobes, it may not be possible to recognize objects or faces at all. Such disorders are called **agnosias**. If you have prosopagnosia, a difficulty in recognizing faces, you may be unable to identify the person with whom you are eating dinner without using cues from their voice and clothing, and if you have an **object agnosia** you may be unable to identify what the food stuff is that you are attempting to eat.

As you continue through your meal, you may want to remember the name of the dish which you are eating, particularly if it appears to bear little relationship to what you thought you had selected. You may also try to remember a joke to amuse your companion. These recollections of previous experiences or knowledge call upon the activity of the temporal lobes. Their underlying structures, the **hippocampi**, are also involved in memory processes. The memory processing in the temporal lobes involves both the verbal description of dishes and the name of your restaurant, and also the recollection of the restaurant's appearance and its whereabouts, so that you are able to find it and recognize it on a subsequent occasion. The right temporal lobe is more involved in the latter process and the left temporal lobe in the former. Thus, the nature of memory organization is affected by the type of information that has to be remembered.

The temporal lobes are also involved in many processes concerned with understanding language. If you listen to the conversation floating across the table of your restaurant and distinguish the voice of the speaker from other voices in the restaurant, your temporal lobes are working hard. When your companion tells you that on a previous occasion he came to this restaurant, ate one of these dishes and was convinced that this restaurant was a better restaurant than it seems on the night that you are sitting there, he is using his temporal lobes to recall this experience, but you are also using your temporal lobes to interpret the dietary information which he is conveying and compare it with similar previous experiences. In some cases of damage to areas around the temporal lobes, you may lose this ability to identify the significance of the words, resulting in a comprehension disorder and leading to a disorder of language, in which you have difficulty in following the message which is being conveyed. This type of disorder includes **Wernicke's aphasia** which was mentioned earlier. In another condition, you may have difficulty in recognizing what any of the words which your companion is saying mean. In these cases of **pure word deafness** or **auditory agnosia**, the words can be clearly heard but no longer sound familiar, the language sounding like a foreign language in which you do not know the vocabulary. These sorts of verbal auditory agnosias may occur following damage to the left temporal lobe. Following damage to the right temporal lobe, you may have difficulty with the identification of environmental noises. The familiar sounds of the waiter approaching your table to make an inquiry about the progress of your meal and the sound of the chairs scraping behind you, indicating that the person moving at the next table is about to bump into you, will not be interpreted appropriately. The ability to understand and interpret these environmental noises is also critical in our day-to-day activity, though we may be less aware and conscious of our use of these processes than of our interpretation of verbal communication.

Listening to the Band: Cerebral Asymmetries

In psychology experiments, people are often interested in the relative skills of the two hemispheres of the brain and they may investigate these by placing them in competition. One way to do this is to use a **dichotic listening technique**, which is based on the principle that the connections from each ear are strongest to the opposite hemisphere and rather weak to the same hemisphere, that is, the right ear is strongly connected to the left-hand side of the brain, but rather weakly connected to the right-hand side, whereas the opposite picture is true for the left ear, with its strongest connection being to the right-hand side of the brain. If the experimenter plays different verbal information into each ear and asks the subject to selectively focus attention on one or other ear, or to record all of the information coming into both ears, subjects show superior performance in recalling verbal information coming into the right ear and musical information coming into the left ear. The temporal lobes are involved in the analysis of these competing information inputs. Sitting in your restaurant, if you are attempting to eavesdrop on an important conversation and you are a right-handed person, it is better to sit with the people having that conversation on your right-hand side. On the other hand, if you are trying to listen to a musical melody which is being played by the band in your restaurant, and for some reason it is vital that you identify the component notes and overall structure of this melody, you may wish to orient your left ear towards it, particularly if there is a competing band in the other corner.

Dividing the Bill: the Frontal Lobes

In planning ahead and thinking about the balance of the different dishes you may want to eat in your meal, where you want to sit and how you can get your companion to change seats with you so that you can listen to the orchestra appropriately, it is necessary to activate your **frontal lobes**. These highly evolved areas of the brain are considered by some to contain our most human capacities. Certainly they are the most recently expanded development in the evolutionary scale in comparison to the other lobes of the brain. They are involved in planning, organization and higher-level executive control systems. At the end of your meal, the frontal lobes are involved in the complex arithmetical calculation which may be involved in the division of the bill. Whilst the basic mechanics of arithmetic involve parietal areas, the organizational processes involved in working out the procedures which have to be conducted are controlled by frontal areas.

As you depart from your restaurant to go on to a party, the frontal lobes may be involved in planning the route that you will take, if it requires several stops on the way: one to pick up another friend; another to collect more alcohol; and a third to drop off somebody from the restaurant who has decided to go home. In attempting to study planning in a controlled situation in the laboratory, Shallice (1982) has employed a Tower of London task. In this task, three pegs are involved of differing lengths (see fig. 2.13). On the first peg one ball can sit, on the second, two, and on the third, three. The balls are coloured differently: red, green and blue. They are placed in a pre-set arrangement across the pegs and the subject is given a card which displays the balls in a different format. The subject has to move the balls to make the arrangement like the target array on the card, but there are certain rules. They can

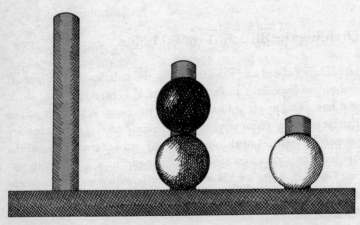

2.13 The Tower of London: Moving one ball at a time the balls must be rearranged to construct an illustrated pattern (Shallice, 1982).

only lift one ball off a peg at a time. Furthermore, they must not put this ball down on the table. Thus, the solution of the task must proceed step by step, moving one ball at a time, to reach the final conclusion. This test assesses the ability to think ahead in planning a sequence of moves. In the more complicated items on the task, it may be necessary to move a ball from one peg to an intermediate peg before it reaches its final position, so that the ball sitting underneath it can be moved appropriately.

The frontal lobes are also involved in the regulation and alteration of plans and actions. If you are driving to your next destination and find that several of the roads have been blocked off because of roadworks so that you have to alter your route, the frontal lobes will be involved in modulating and altering the course of action which you were taking. Frequently, patients with frontal lobe damage will correctly say that they have noted something about their behaviour which is not working, but will have difficulty in incorporating this correction into their plan. If they make a mistake in finding the route through a maze and are told about it, they may agree about the error; yet, when they start at the beginning and go through the maze again, they may repeat exactly the same error. They are said to be inflexible, showing rigidity of thought and lack of adaptability.

As you arrive at your party and enter the house, your conversation with your host or hostess and the nature of the conversation which you have with those around you will be modulated by the social relationships of these people. If they are business colleagues, your behaviour will be different from if they are close friends. These processes of social awareness and social inhibition are also under the control of the frontal lobes. As you have a late-night drink, their effects may be less considerable as you become disinhibited.

Further laboratory tests illustrate other examples of behaviours under the control of the frontal lobes. If you are requested to name as many animals as you can in a minute or to hunt out words in your vocabulary falling into some other category, the frontal lobes are involved in those search-and-retrieval strategies. They affect your **verbal fluency**. Their involvement in adaptation to unusual situations with verbal material is illustrated with the **stroop task**. One format of this task consists of a set of four cards. On one there are colour names, written in black and white ink. On another there are sets of coloured crosses, in which the colours have to be named. There is also a card in which colour names are written in the colour of the name. Thus, the word 'green' is written in green ink and the word 'blue' in blue ink. Finally there is an incongruent card with a lack of match between the colour name and the colour of the ink. So, for example, the word 'green' may be written in red ink and the word 'red' written in blue ink. Comparing the rapidity in naming the coloured inks in congruent and incongruent conditions or in incongruent and neutral conditions assesses the level of interference and distraction created by the competing colour name. Frontal-lobe patients are said to show an exaggerated degree of distraction in this task, which is called an exaggerated **stroop effect**.

Another clinical test which involves the use of cards with colours assesses the ability to shift rapidly from one concept to

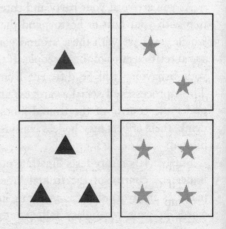

2.14 Target cards used in the Wisconsin Card Sorting Test: Their patterns vary in colour, shape and number.

another. On the Winconsin Card Sorting Test, there are four target cards (see fig. 2.14). These contain one red triangle, two yellow stars, three blue triangles and four yellow stars. Thus, the cards vary in colour, number and form. The subject is given a pack of cards varying on all three dimensions and is requested to match each of the cards in the pack with one of the target cards. They are given feedback on each match as to whether it is correct or incorrect. The subject must work out the sorting principle which is being applied. In the first instance this is colour. If the subject correctly places a blue card by a blue card, they are told 'yes', and if they match according to any other dimension, that is, by number, by shape, or by no principle at all, then they are told that they are incorrect. However, after they have sorted correctly ten times, the sorting principle is altered without the subject being informed. The sorting principle applied is then shape. When the subject matches correctly, according to shape, they are told they are correct, otherwise they are told they are incorrect. Subsequently, in the same way, the sorting principle is changed to number and so it continues. Patients who have frontal injuries have difficulty in making this sort of conceptual shift. They will continue to persevere sorting according to the previous sorting principle, even though they are continually told that this is incorrect. The impairment does not appear to arise because of any failure to distinguish the three different dimensions which are relevant. When asked at the end of the task how these cards vary, the patients may be able to say that they vary according to colour, shape and number. Yet they seem to have difficulty in altering an on-going method of solving a problem in response to a changing situation.

This inflexibility of thought is also displayed on perceptual tasks, such as the double Necker cube (see fig. 2.15), which has a reversible perspective and can be seen in one of two ways. Typically, if you stare at this picture, after a period of time it appears to jump from one perspective to another. However, frontal lobe patients tend not to see these switches with the same rapidity.

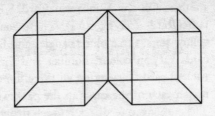

2.15 A double Necker cube: The frontal lobes are believed to be involved in the reversals of perspective which occur as the pattern is studied.

The assessment of more complex planning and organizational skills has been harder for psychologists to test. Some frontal patients appear to pass all the laboratory frontal tests, yet have blatantly severe deficits in the organization of their day-to-day life and activities. One researcher addressed such problems by setting the patients shopping tasks in the local mall, and then had them tailed by research assistants who were recording their movements. For many obvious reasons this is unlikely to catch on as a universal paradigm.

The quest to localize functions in different regions of the brain has flowed and ebbed. Traditional neuropsychologists have been interested in mapping functional deficits to neurological lesion locations. However, amongst contemporary approaches, **cognitive neuropsychologists** have argued that a good model of how a system works is more important than where it is found. Cognitive neuropsychologists look at the dissociations in the ease and difficulty which neurological patients encounter on different tasks. They argue that these provide information about the component **modules** (Foder, 1983) of thinking processes and how they are connected. This contributes to models of normal cognitive processes and also enables an explanation for the patient's behaviour which is grounded in testable theory.

Chapter Three
The Corpus Callosum

If you were able to remove your skull and look at your brain in the mirror, you would notice immediately that it is made up of two approximately symmetrical hemispheric structures. These two cerebral hemispheres are interconnected by several **commissural** fibre tracts, the largest of which is the **corpus callosum** which contains two hundred million nerve fibres. You cannot see the corpus callosum from the outside but it would be very conspicuous if you were able to look at the inner surface of the brain (see fig. 3.1 and 3.2). It is white in appearance and is four to six centimetres in length. Each fibre within the corpus callosum departs from one hemisphere of the brain and arrives in the other, making no synaptic connections in between which means that some of the fibres within the corpus callosum are particularly long in relation to the axonal length of other fibres in the human brain.

Mirror-image points tend to be connected through the corpus callosum. For example, the frontal lobe on one side of the brain connects with the frontal lobe on the other side. Within the corpus callosum there is further fine topographical organization (see fig. 3.3). Moving a few fibres forwards or backwards along the fibre tract, the corresponding area of interconnection moves forward or back.

Two other commissural fibre tracts are the **anterior commissure** and the **hippocampal commissure**, but these are significantly smaller than the corpus callosum. The anterior commissure carries only five per cent of the fibres of the corpus callosum.

Fibre tracts form in sequential order during embryological

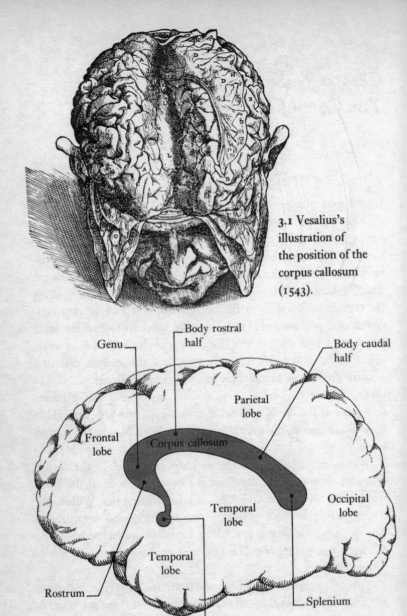

3.1 Vesalius's illustration of the position of the corpus callosum (1543).

3.2 The areas of the corpus callosum and its interconnections.

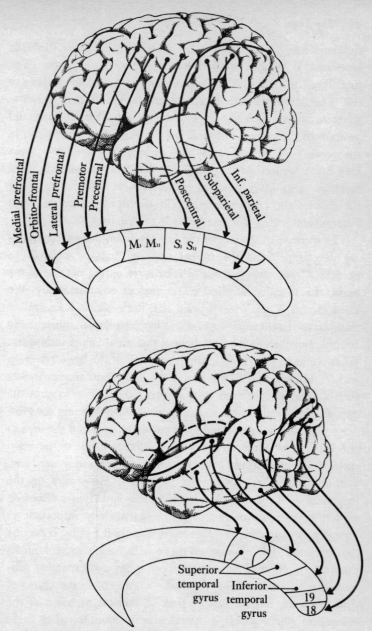

Medial prefrontal
Orbito-frontal
Lateral prefrontal
Premotor
Precentral
Postcentral
Subparietal
Inf. parietal

M₁ M₁₁ S₁ S₁₁

Superior
temporal
gyrus
Inferior
temporal
gyrus
19
18

3.3 Probable topographic organization of the corpus callosum:
extrapolated from primate studies.

development: the anterior commissure forming first, then the hippocampal commissure and finally the corpus callosum. The first fibres of the corpus callosum cross from one hemisphere to the other during foetal development, around weeks twelve to thirteen; by weeks eighteen to twenty, the overall shape and position of the corpus callosum is as in the adult. Disruption in the process of embryological development during these weeks may cause failure in the formation of the corpus callosum. The resultant cases of **callosal agenesis** provide information about the role of the corpus callosum in the development of brain function and will be discussed later in this chapter.

The increase in the size of the human brain, during evolutionary development up the animal kingdom, can be charted. In particular, the volume of the cellular layer on the outside of the brain, the so-called cerebral cortex, increases substantially. We know that it is not overall brain size itself which is critical in relation to intellectual capacity. Elephants have substantially larger brains than man yet we believe that we are more intelligent. What seems to be critical is the proportion of the brain taken up with cerebral cortex. This thin layer of cortical tissue reaches such a great size in man that, in order to fit it in around the outside of the brain, it has to bend up and down forming convolutions, dips and bumps. Bumps are known as **gyri** and the dips as **sulci**. If the human cortex was taken off the outside of the brain and spread out, it would cover the area of a moderately sized rug. Within the cerebral cortex, the proportion that makes up the frontal lobes of the brain has increased particularly. As discussed earlier, these areas of the brain are particularly important in planning, organization and higher-level reasoning skills; it may be the increased development of these skills which gives humans their true intellect. The corpus callosum has also expanded substantially in humans. This fibre tract is present in the brains of many animals, but reaches its peak in humans in terms of the volume of fibres which it contains in relation to other brain structures. The ratio of the cross-sectional area of the corpus

Species	Index	
Man	3.12	
Chimpanzee	1.79	
Baboon	1.39	
Guenon	1.19	
Elephant	1.11	
Brown bear	1.07	
Polar bear	1.06	The calloso-bulbar index is the ratio
Dolphin	0.93	of the number of collosal fibres di-
Wolf	0.89	vided by the number of ascending
Horse	0.70	and descending brainstem fibres.
Lion	0.67	Source: Blinkov, S. M. and Glezer,
Fox	0.62	I. I. (1968) *The Human Brain in*
Hippopotamus	0.56	*Figures and Tables*, Plenum Press,
Lemur	0.32	New York.

3.4 The ratio of the cross-sectional area of the corpus callosum to the brain stem.

callosum to the cross-sectional area of the brain stem is given in fig. 3.4 for several species. This striking evolutionary development suggests that the corpus callosum plays a critical role in human behaviour.

It is now recognized that the corpus callosum does play an important role in brain function and organization. However, it was not always perceived in this light. The history of the corpus callosum has been chequered. At its lowest ebb, it was seen as a structure that simply holds the two halves of the brain together to stop them falling apart into the inner sides of the skull. Vesalius, writing in the sixteenth century, believed that the corpus callosum functioned mainly as a mechanical support. Although this idea might seem improbable, it was prevalent as recently as the beginning of this century. In its greater heyday the corpus callosum was considered to be the seat of the soul. It was thought that its complex fibre connections and well-protected location gave it a clear advantage in the capacity to integrate sensory experience and emotion. Recent experiments have highlighted how, without the corpus callosum, sensory experience is not fully integrated. Yet it is clear that, even in the absence of a corpus callosum, individuals are not rendered without 'soul' or without human capacities.

The most informative evidence of the role of the corpus callosum in human skills and abilities comes in the treatment of intractable epilepsy, from studies of neurological patients whose corpus callosum has been cut during an operation with therapeutic objectives. The range and diversity of the callosal functions are seen in studies of these so called 'split-brain' patients, more formally referred to as 'commissurotomy' patients.

Nowadays epilepsy, in most cases, is not a severely handicapping condition and can be well controlled by drugs and medication. However, in some unfortunate individuals, the seizures do not respond well to medication, and in some of these cases surgical intervention has been attempted. It is not fully understood why sectioning of the corpus callosum should be effective in the reduction of seizure frequency in epilepsy. One could understand the logic if the operation somehow stopped the epileptic seizure spreading from one half of the brain through to the other half, but it is not clear why the seizures should stop altogether. It is a further surprise that, whereas sectioning of the corpus callosum can cause the reduction of seizure frequency in epilepsy, the most common neurological complication of callosal agenesis, in which children are born without the corpus callosum, is epilepsy itself. Thus, in one patient group, epilepsy is rendered less likely, in the other, more likely. It is probable that in cases of callosal agenesis it is not absence of the corpus callosum *per se* which causes the epilepsy, but rather some other concomitant brain disorder.

Early studies showed that split-brain patients might have no side effects from their operation; evidence from other neurological patients in whom the corpus callosum had been damaged by tumour, infarction or degenerative disease confirmed this view.

However, subsequent, more detailed, neuropsychological invest-igations revealed some striking effects of cerebral disconnection. This work showed in detail the extensive functional asymmetries of the two cerebral hemispheres of the brain and their different specializations. Sperry received a Nobel prize for some of the work and split-brain experiments continue to interest psycholo-gists, philosophers, linguists and journalists.

At the end of the 1890s Broca had brought to the attention of the scientific community the association which he had observed in his neurological patients between disorders of language produc-tion and damage to the third frontal area of the left-hand side of the brain. The left hemisphere was seen to be dominant for language. The extent of this dominance is particularly evident in the studies of split-brain patients. In these patients the sectioning of the corpus callosum meant that the language systems of the left hemisphere were inaccessible to the functional activities of the right hemisphere and *vice versa*. In everyday conversation the effects of these disconnections might not be apparent, but with specialized presentation of material, the extent of the abnormal disconnection was clear (e.g. Sperry, 1970).

In order to understand the various split-brain studies, it is worth checking the wiring diagram of the body. Firstly, each hand of the body is controlled by the opposite side of the brain, thus, the right hand is controlled by the left hemisphere and the left hand is controlled by the right hemisphere. This lateralized control extends to the whole of the opposite side of the body, but for the experiments to be described here, it is the control of hand use which is critical. This control extends both to the interpreta-tion of sensory information, as input to the body, and the control of movements and motor output from the body. So, if an object or shape is put in the left hand, it is the right hemisphere which feels the structure and may move it (see fig. 3.5).

Not only is there crossing of fibres from the limbs of the body, there is also crossing of fibres in the visual system. It is not the case that the right eye is connected with the left half of the

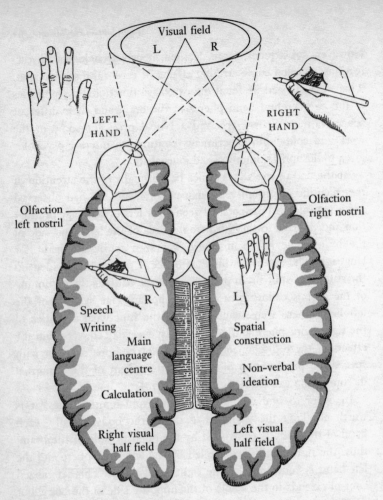

3.5 Lateralization in the cerebral cortex.

brain and the left eye with the right half of the brain, rather it is the right visual field which connects to the left half of the brain. This means that if you look straight ahead at a screen, at a central point, everything to the right-hand side of that point, that is, everything on the right-hand side of the world, is projected initially to the left-hand side of the brain, whilst everything on the left-hand side of the world is connected to the right-hand side

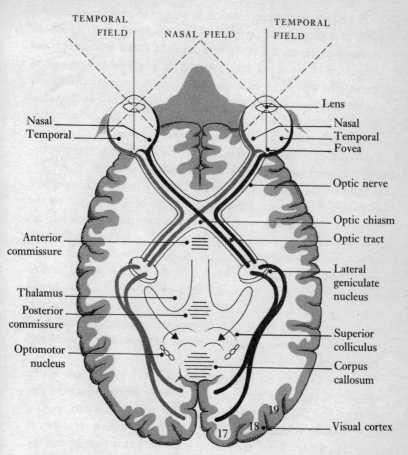

3.6 The connections of the eyes.

of the brain. Thus, both eyes connect with each half of the brain, but only one half of the visual world does (see fig. 3.6). Normally as we are walking around, we move our eyes and so both halves of the brain have access to visual information. Further, there is normally an exchange of this visual information across the posterior area of the corpus callosum, known as the **splenium**. In split-brain patients, the integration of visual information across the splenium is not possible.

If we restrict the presentation of visual information to about a tenth of a second, the time frame is not long enough to allow us to move our eyes. So, if we look straight ahead at a screen and something is presented for one-tenth of a second to one side of the screen, that is, in one visual field, then there is no time for the eyes to move and we can restrict the initial input of the visual information to one hemisphere of the brain. This type of presentation is referred to as a **tachistoscopic presentation** and is a methodology which is used in many areas of experimental psychology, as well as in studies of neurological patients. Normally, despite tachistoscopic presentation, the unstimulated hemisphere of the brain will gain subsequent access to the information via the corpus callosum, but in split-brain patients the information remains isolated in one hemisphere. Using a tachistoscope with split-brain patients, it is possible, to present things in the right visual field which only the left hemisphere is able to see, and to present things in the left visual field which only the right hemisphere is able to see. These two basic pieces of information, about the way the hands and the eyes are wired up, are sufficient to account for several major oddities of behaviour seen in the performance of split-brain patients.

One of the most striking phenomena which can be seen in the split-brain patient is the incapacity to name objects which are put in the left hand out of sight. So, if the patient is asked to shut their eyes or is blindfolded, and a pencil, or a fork, or a key is placed in the left hand, the patient is unable to say the name of the object. This difficulty in naming is referred to as an **anomia** and, since it only occurs with objects in the left hand, is referred to as a **unimanual anomia**. The explanation for this difficulty is that the left hand is connected with the right hemisphere of the brain and this right hemisphere does not have access to the naming skills of language. These skills are located in the left hemisphere. The left hemisphere knows about the names of things and the right hemisphere (connected to the left hand) knows about the identity of the object. But these two pieces of information cannot connect. This type of effect in the split-brain patients is therefore called a **disconnection effect**. When exactly the same object is placed in the right hand, the patient can very easily identify it. This hand has direct connections to the left hemisphere and, therefore, language centres which means that naming is now possible.

Whilst a number of the characteristics of the commissurotomy syndrome recede with the passage of years, unimanual anomia is particularly resistant to any sort of change or improvement. A similar phenomenon is evident if a picture of an object or a creature, like a banana or frog, is presented via the tachistoscope in the left visual field of the subject (see fig. 3.7). As explained

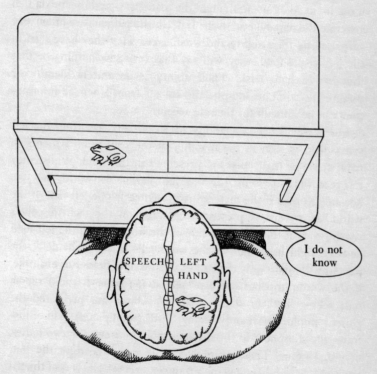

3.7 A disconnection effect: The right hemisphere has seen the frog but cannot access the name 'frog' from the left hemisphere.

above, if presentation is brief this can restrict the input to the right hemisphere of the brain. The patient is unable to name objects or creatures presented in this way though they are able to name comparable items presented in the right visual field.

We know that the naming difficulties within the left visual field are not difficulties in recognizing the items, that is, identifying a frog or a banana, because the patient is able to match pictures presented in the left visual field with objects felt with the left hand, and is able to gesture the use of the object. So, for example, if a picture of a bunch of keys was presented in the left visual field, the left hand would be able to mime how keys are used in a door, even though the patient would be unable to generate the name 'keys' itself. Indeed, the patients are often very surprised by their ability and when asked what they have seen in the left visual field, they will say that they saw nothing or that they saw a light flash. Their ability to accurately identify or gesture the stimulus, despite the cut-off from language information, can be difficult for them to accept.

Further evidence of inability to access language from the left visual field is seen in the inability of the split-brain patients to read words or digits that are presented in this field. Whilst they can read words presented in the right half of the world, they are not able to read if the material is presented in the left half of the world. If a word is presented centrally on the tachistoscope's screen, so that the left-hand side of the word falls in the left field and the right-hand side of the word falls in the right field, the patient will report only the half in the the right field. For example, if the words 'top hat' were presented the patient would report only seeing 'hat', or if the word 'blackbird' was presented the patient would report only seeing 'bird' (see fig. 3.8). This illustrates the sharpness of the disconnection between the two halves of visual input. These examples all illustrate the difficulty that the right hemisphere has in producing verbal labels and verbal information.

A further range of 'disconnection' effects involving language

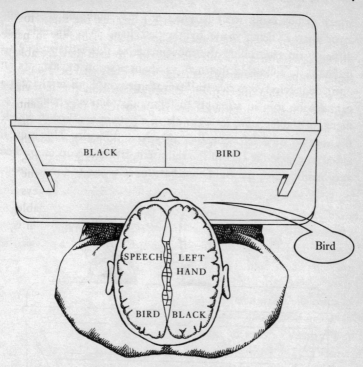

3.8 A disconnection effect: The left hemisphere responds with speech only to the word seen on the right of the screen.

occurs if the right hemisphere is asked to follow verbal information or instructions. One way in which this can be done is to ask the patient verbally to make particular movements with the left hand. Since the control of the left hand is from the right hemisphere, by asking the left hand to do something, we are effectively asking the right hemisphere to do it. If we ask the right hemisphere 'touch your nose with your left hand' the patient may fail, instead perhaps moving the left hand up to the mouth. It is possible to check that the patient has heard the instruction clearly and has verbally understood it. They are able to repeat the instruction and the language half of the brain (that is, the left hemisphere, which is observing what is going on) may note and detect the error that is being made by the left hand. Yet there is still difficulty in controlling the movements of this left hand. This difficulty in following instructions about a set of movements on one side is referred to as a **unilateral apraxia**. Unilateral apraxia can also be seen in attempts to follow instructions about movements of the feet. So, for example, if a patient is asked to wiggle the toes on their left foot, they may have difficulty. However, if asked to wiggle the toes of the right foot, the task is accomplished very easily, since the right foot has direct access to the language

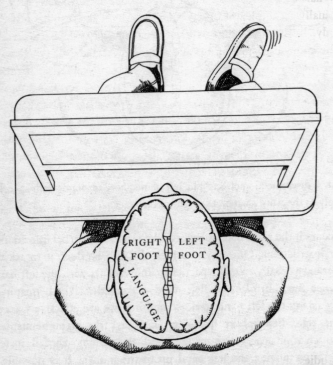

3.9 Unilateral apraxia: Verbal instructions to the right-hand side of the body are followed but with the left-hand side of the body the patient has difficulty.

areas of the left hemisphere and therefore understands the instructions which have been given (see fig. 3.9). Over time, after the operation, the patient's degree of unilateral apraxia tends to recede; it is a symptom that is seen in a less and less extreme form in patients many years after the operation.

In addition to the difficulty in controlling hand movements in response to verbal instruction, there is also difficulty in controlling the hand movements which are to be used for spelling and writing. This difficulty occurs both in spelling to dictation and in spontaneous writing and spelling. Of course, most right handers find it hard to write with the left hand but nevertheless they can usually accomplish it to some degree even if the result is less than tidy. In the split-brain patients the language systems involved in the control of spelling output are disconnected from the control of the left hand. This results in what is called **unimanual agraphia**. So if you ask the patient to write a set of words with the right hand, they may be able to write them quite easily and efficiently. If the left hand is asked to write the same words, the patient produces an incomprehensible scrawl. In the case of these patients, the problem is very much more extreme than it would be in normal right handers. It is not just that the letters are poorly written and rather badly structured but the individual letters are not produced at all. This is a symptom in which there are some individual differences between the patients, but the general result is seen in many cases.

These studies provide further evidence of the left hemisphere's role in language. However, it would be wrong to imply that split-brain patients are always better at doing things with their right hand, or at carrying out tasks where information is presented to the right visual field. These biases are only found for tasks that necessitate the use of language. In a series of other tasks and studies, it can be shown that the right hemisphere of the brain is better than the left at processing other sorts of information and so biases can be seen in the reverse direction. For example, if pictures of faces are presented in either the left field or the right field of the tachistoscope, performance is higher with left-field presentation. The right hemisphere is better at recognizing the faces than the left which does it less efficiently and possibly in a different way.

The left hand is better at doing jigsaws and puzzles and at organizing shapes and patterns than the right hand; this may reflect the superiority of the right hemisphere in certain visuospatial skills. In normal right handers there can be a slight advantage of the left hand in making tactile judgements and arranging puzzles but in split-brain patients the difference in the performance of the hands is much more extreme.

The right hemisphere also seems to have a better sense of humour than the left. It is more ready to see a joke and may be more emotional. This can be seen in the patient's response to cartoons or humorous situations presented in one or other visual field. In the classic anecdote the patient is looking at pictures of objects in either visual field and a picture of a nude is projected to the left visual field. The patient blushes and giggles, displaying clearly that they have recognized the picture but they are unable to say what has triggered the response. The same degree of emotion and humour is not triggered when the nude is presented in the right visual field and the left hemisphere verbally identifies it.

There has been much interest in whether the right brain has any language at all and it seems that in many people it does have some language capacities, but that these are restricted and of a particular sort. Detailed testing of the right hemisphere of the split-brain patients indicates that this half of the brain can deal with some basic vocabulary but is very poor at grammar and at linking words together. It may have some understanding of the meaning of words but does not use codes that are based upon the sound of words and, therefore, has poor **phonological skills** (Zaidel, 1978).

Most of the studies of the split-brain patients have involved looking at how they do things with either visual material or the identification of tactile material. However, further disconnections are found in other sensory modalities – for example, olfaction.

Unlike the eyes, the ears and the hands, the sensory connections for the nose are uncrossed. The right nostril connects to the right brain and the left nostril to the left brain. A disconnection effect appears if a particular scent is presented to the right nostril and the patient is asked to name it. For example, if the left nostril is held closed and the patient is asked to identify a fishy smell with the right nostril, they have difficulty. It is not that the smell has not been identified, since with the left hand they will be able to select a plastic fish from an array. The split-brain patients have difficulty with any task in which the stimulus and response are controlled by different halves of the brain.

Further studies indicate that each half of the brain is capable of making a decision independently of the other and, indeed, even at the same time. One illustration of this is studies using what are called **chimeric faces** (see fig. 3.10). These faces are made by taking front-view photographs of faces and sectioning them top to bottom between the eyes, and bisecting the nose and the mouth, producing a left-hand side of a face and a right-hand side of a face. The left-hand side of the face can be combined with a different right-hand side to produce strange faces, in which each

3.10 Chimeric faces.

half-face comes from a different person. Using the whole faces from which the chimeric faces were made, the split-brain patient can be taught the names of particular people. Thus, one face can be labelled John, another William and another Thomas, et cetera. The chimeric faces can then be presented on a tachistoscope with the mid-line junction at the centre of the visual field. In this way, one half-face is presented to the right brain and one half-face to the left brain. One can then test the patient by asking them whose face they saw. If we ask for a verbal reply, that is, what the name of the face is, then the patient will name the face that was seen in the right field. However, if we ask the patient to point with the left hand to the face that was seen, then the patient will point to the face that was seen in the left field. It is possible to ask for both of these responses at the same time and to get two different responses. This pattern of performance confirms observations from the animal literature on work done on monkeys, in which split-brain monkeys could learn two differing and conflicting solutions to the same problem, with one being learned in each half of the brain.

It could be anticipated that this capacity of each half of the brain to make an independent decision might cause problems for the split-brain patients in their everyday life, since potentially two simultaneous and conflicting decisions could be made at once. In practice, it appears that the number of situations in which there is overt conflict are limited, but when they are seen they are very conspicuous in quality and may be dramatic a short time after surgery. For example, in one well-documented patient, there is a description of his right hand buttoning up his shirt whilst his left hand comes along behind and unbuttons the shirt. Female patients also report conflict, where they may reach into their wardrobe and each hand may select a different dress to wear at the same time. There is also a description of a split-brain patient shopping for herself and her daughter in the supermarket. The lady preferred pastry filled with a particular fruit, whilst her daughter preferred a different fruit. She found one of her hands, the left, stretching for the fruit pastry which she herself liked and the right hand stretching for the fruit pastry which her daughter liked. The two hands got into conflict in the freezer compartment, leading to extremely long delays in making decisions so that it would take several hours to complete a simple shopping trip (Ferguson, Rayport and Corrie, 1988). More common conflicts may arise in dissociations between what the patient is saying and what the left hand is doing. This was illustrated in the chimeric faces experiment, but can also be seen in day-to-day situations. There may also be situations where there is a discrepancy between the expression on the patient's face, a process more dominantly controlled by the right brain, and the patient's verbalization of their emotional state. In general, split-brain patients engage in little verbal discussion of their emotional states.

These discrepancies between the decisions made in the two halves of the brain and the subsequent conflicts, along with the inaccessibility of the right hemisphere's decisions to language, have been of much interest to philosophers. They have been interested in the results, both in relation to the integration of consciousness and what is meant by man's mind and humanity. They have also been interested in the inaccessibility of some decision-making to verbal and rational output in discussion. This has led those with a psychoanalytical bent to locate some of the subconscious processes in the right hemisphere. However, the validity of this would be disputed by many today.

The brain-damaged patients we have been discussing had the corpus callosum sectioned in adulthood. Their brains were able to grow and develop with the corpus callosum, and the fibre tract was sectioned after all their adult cognitive systems had become established. These patients can tell us about the role of this fibre tract in active processing of the two halves of the brain, but they cannot tell us anything about the role of the corpus callosum in the development of brain function. There is another syndrome, which has been less extensively investigated, in which children are born without the corpus callosum. This syndrome is referred to as **callosal agenesis** or agenesis of the corpus callosum and the patients are often referred to as **acallosals**. In callosal agenesis, there is congenital absence of the 200,000,000 fibres which form the corpus callosum and the syndrome can provide information about the role of the corpus callosum in the development of cognitive function.

In children with callosal agenesis there is some disruption to the process of embryological development of the growth of the corpus callosum. In the most common form of the condition, there is total absence of the corpus callosum and of the hippocampal commissure, but the anterior commissure is preserved. In other cases the anterior commissure is also absent. The origins of callosal agenesis are not known. In some cases there is a genetic mechanism and both dominant and recessive modes of transmission have been described. However, it has also been suggested that exposure to toxins or biochemical disturbance, at a critical phase in foetal development, may also disrupt growth of the fibre tract.

Callosal agenesis is a very rare neurological disorder in children; in the scientific literature fewer than 300 cases have been described. In many of these cases, there is other brain pathology which means that, in many of the original case descriptions, children were described who had general learning disabilities. However, we now know that children with callosal agenesis need not have general learning disabilities; it is simply that children with other forms of mental impairment may be more likely to receive the brain scans which are necessary for the diagnosis of the condition. Thus, the neurological literature is distorted by the presence of children with other neurological abnormalities.

In the brains of all children with callosal agenesis, there are some other unusual features. The anterior commissure is bigger than usual and carries a tiny percentage of the fibres that would normally cross in the corpus callosum. This may aid in some of the compensation that we see in these children. There is also an unusual fibre tract found in the acallosal children which is referred to as **Probst's bundle**. This contains many of the fibres that would normally cross through the corpus callosum from one half of the brain to the other but which instead are passing from front to back and back to front of the brain, along the medial wall of the hemispheres. Thus, some of the fibres that would normally have grown *across* the brain are instead growing *down* the medial wall. It is not clear what function Probst's bundle plays and, indeed, whether acallosal children may be capable of some function which normal people are not capable of, since normal people do not have this distinctive fibre connection.

The absence of the corpus callosum in the brains of acallosal children causes certain brain structures to sit in different positions from normal. In particular, the **lateral ventricles**, two of the fluid-filled cavities within the brain, sit in a higher position than normal. This produces a characteristic image on brain scan which is used in the diagnosis of callosal agenesis. There are suggestions of other minor abnormalities in the brains of children with callosal agenesis, relating to the patterning of the sulci or gyri and the possible absence of some pyramidal cells in layers of projection for the corpus callosum.

Children with normal intelligence and callosal agenesis provide the opportunity to study the role of this fibre tract in the normal development of different skills and abilities in children. In particular, if the corpus callosum is critical for the development of any particular function, then difficulties with that skill should be seen in each and every child with callosal agenesis. Whilst the split-brain patients discussed earlier can provide information about what the corpus callosum may be doing minute by minute during thinking, these studies of adults cannot tell us anything about what the corpus callosum might have been doing when different functions were being developed and being learnt. In the children with callosal agenesis the fibre tract is absent from birth, so any systems which develop in the brain are doing so in the absence of this normal set of neuronal connections.

It was suggested that the corpus callosum might be essential for the normal development of lateralization of language to the left hemisphere of the brain. It was thought that the corpus callosum might be involved in switching off one half of the brain and inhibiting its development of language, leading to the asymmetry of function that was discussed earlier. However, studies of acallosal children and adults do not support this view. In dichotic listening studies and studies using lateralized tachistoscopic presentation, it is seen that there is normal lateralization of language to the left hemisphere in most acallosals. Studies of infants now suggest that the direction of lateralization is already specified at birth or in the early neonatal period. It is still possible that its extent and the extremity of the asymmetry become greater as children grow up, and it may be that children with callosal agenesis will show less extreme differences between the two halves of their brain in relation to their functions than would normally be seen in other children.

A second issue that has been raised is whether the corpus callosum is essential for the development of any specific cognitive function. There have only been a limited number of studies addressing this question and they have tended to focus on the domain of language. In 1981 Dennis suggested, following a study of one of her patients with callosal agenesis, that the corpus callosum might be critical in order to develop certain grammatical skills and the ability to use language in a general social context. In a subsequent re-analysis of her data by Jeeves and Temple (1987), the conclusion which Dennis drew was questioned. They suggested that her patient actually had a problem with some of the sound-based elements of language required in explicit phonological processing. In Dennis's study, these skills were used in certain rhyming tasks and also in attempting to retrieve words from initial-letter cues. In a typical fluency task of this sort, the patient is asked to generate as many words as they can beginning, say, with the letter 's'. The patient is given a minute to do this and the number of words produced gives some measure not only of vocabulary levels, but also of the ease with which words can be accessed from the vocabulary to sound-based cues. As a comparable measure the subjects are asked to retrieve as many words as they can, in particular semantic categories. For example, they may be asked to retrieve the names of animals. If the problem is in accessing vocabulary from phonological cues, but there is not a general problem with vocabulary or fluency, then there will be low scores on the initial-letter fluency sections but normal scores on the semantic category fluency sections. This is the case in the subject with callosal agenesis studied by Dennis. Dennis's patient had no difficulty in retrieving names and vocabulary in picture-naming tasks, but did have difficulty on initial-letter fluency tasks. Subsequently, in collaboration with Professor Malcolm Jeeves at the University of St Andrews, we have in our own lab investigated further cases of callosal agenesis. We found that difficulty with sound-based elements of language and explicit phonological processing was widespread across these subjects, who had difficulty on several different types of rhyming tasks (Temple, Jeeves and Vilarroya 1989). These are evident quite early and also persist into adulthood.

We were particularly interested in this problem because it has been suggested that difficulty with explicit phonological process-ing, such as rhyming, may be a cause of developmental dyslexia. We were interested to know whether our acallosal children with rhyming problems would also have developmental dyslexia, there-fore, we investigated their reading in detail. We found that their reading level as assessed by the ability to recognize familiar written words was normal. A more detailed investigation of their pattern of reading performance showed that they had difficulty with the phonological reading route (Temple, Jeeves and Vilarroya 1990), which will be discussed in a later chapter, but which is used to sound aloud non-words which are pronounceable and also to work out the pronunciation of unfamiliar words. These studies led us to conclude that the corpus callosum may be critical in the normal development of explicit phonological skills.

In some ways this is a surprising result, since our understanding of the asymmetries of language in the brain would suggest that phonological processes are skills very much associated with the left hemisphere of the brain, at least in most right handers. There is no obvious reason why the corpus callosum should be critical in conducting such tasks. We therefore speculated that perhaps the corpus callosum is involved in developing some of the extreme elements of lateralized functions. Alternatively, there may be something about the processing of speech-sound information in response to auditory input, which is abnormal in these cases. Another possibility is that the corpus callosum is necessary, second by second, in order to carry out a rhyming task or a sound-based task, perhaps because of the importance of certain inhibitory inputs. If this were the case then the patients who have had split-brain surgery, who were discussed above, should also have difficulty on rhyming tasks.

There are also suggestions that in callosal agenesis there may be particular impairments in certain forms of spatial skill. Our own studies suggest difficulties with spatial skills with constructional components such as jigsaws, drawing and copying (Temple and Ilsley, 1993). There are other general problems with motor control. Poor bi-manual coordination may have impact as clumsiness in the classroom; in craft; in skills requiring rapid coordination of the hands; on typewriting and playing the piano; and in certain sports.

With relation to processing sensory inputs, there is evidence that children with callosal agensis may have difficulty in resolving fine-grained sensory information, which is presented in a spatial array. An example of such a difficulty would be the ability to interpret particular letters or shapes that are traced out on the palm of the hand, which necessitates analysis of the different positions that are being touched and then interpretation in some spatial way.

There is a debate over the accuracy of depth perception. Practically, when they are observed, it is clear that some are unable to detect depth in a conventional way and use peripheral cues. For example, when I was walking along the road with one acallosal girl, it was noticeable that she stepped down when the tarmac changed to a darker colour and, when this was an inappropriate response, she tripped. Yet there is no real anatomical reason why the corpus callosum ought to be essential for processing depth information, since this information is cross-connected through the optic chiasm which is intact.

Split-brain patients are reported as having impairments in memory; difficulties with memory are also complained of by the parents of children with callosal agenesis. Our initial investigations of memory in these subjects shows that they have particular difficulty with spatial memory, but no obvious difficulty with verbal memory. This is a surprisingly lateralized effect to arrive from a pathology which has a physically central location in the brain. As more subjects with callosal agenesis are seen, and as scanning techniques become more routine, we may anticipate the resolution of the consistency of these deficits and exactly how we should understand this unusual but informative developmental condition.

Chapter Four :
Language and the Brain

Language is a system of communication which enables us to link our experience and knowledge with those of others. For many people, communicating with language is a positive experience in itself; hence friends and neighbours will call in for a chat without necessarily having specific information which they wish to communicate. People also like to gather in groups, and a considerable amount of social activity consists of the exchange via language of differing ideas and news. In a wider sense, language contributes to our cultural life by enabling us to both construct and enjoy works of literature, plays, films and stories. These may be recorded and experienced by generations that differ from the generation who created them.

The importance which we, as a culture, assign to the transmission of factual information from one generation to the next is evident in the time which we allocate for the education of our children by oral communication from teachers. Universities, evening classes and courses of formal instruction may extend this factual transmission process. The prevalence of bookshops, libraries, newspapers, keyboards and faxes provides further evidence of the crucial role of the written word in our society which we will discuss more in Chapter Seven. In general, when we listen to people communicating we also look at them and integrate their gestural and non-verbal communication with their spoken language, but we are also able to understand language in a form detached from a human presence. Thus, we listen to radios. Our dependence upon and addiction to the telephone is apparent in the increased popularity of both car telephones and portable telephones. When people's telephones are out of order for a brief period of time, they will frequently say that they feel isolated from the world. In a broad range of human activities, language plays a central role upon which we have great dependence.

The relationship between language and thought has been debated by philosophers. Those arguing for **mentalism** claim that language expresses an underlying thought which has an independent existence prior to its expression in language, for example, as an idea, an image, a concept or a motivation. In contrast, **materialism** claims that thought is subvocal speech and that thought cannot exist independent of language. These two different perspectives lead us to analyse different components of language in attempting to understand it. Materialism leads to the analysis of the publicly observed side of language, whereas mentalism leads to the analysis of the intellectual and motivational content of speech.

The human brain controls the systems which are involved in both the production and the comprehension of language. It actively analyses and synthesizes language and also stores our knowledge about language and communication. Studies of structural linguistics attempt to understand the way in which the brain does this by analysing the components of sound and grammar which are involved in the production and perception of language, attaching lesser significance to the meaning and message which is being conveyed.

Structural Linguistics

The **articulatory system** controls the movements of the speech musculature which are necessary to produce the sequence of sounds that comprise the particular message. One can divide the language systems which are involved in the brain prior to this into three broad areas: syntactic, semantic and phonological. Broadly speaking, the **syntactic system** is involved with the grammar of a language; the **semantic system** is involved with the individual meanings of words and the **phonological system** is involved with the pronunciation which has to be attached to messages. In addition, a **prosodic system** will alter the intonation which is attached to utterances which may in turn alter the meaning of the message. Thus, for example, the communication 'it's raining' might generally be spoken in a tone of voice indicating displeasure. However, if there had been a recent drought or if you are a gardening enthusiast, the same utterance could be expressed with different emphasis indicating enthusiasm. Thus, some of the emotional content of messages is conveyed, not by the specific words and grammar which are involved, but by the nature of the prosodic elements which are added to the communication. Finally, because language is part of a social communication system, there are *pragmatic* components which place further constraints. If, at the dinner table, you ask the host whether he has any salt, you do not require the answer 'yes' or 'no', but you are indicating that you would like to receive some salt, even though this is not explicitly stated in what you have said.

In producing language, the brain must integrate all of these systems in order to produce a continuous flow of speech. Similarly, in perceiving language, the brain must decompose the elements of the language it hears, in order to extract the message which is being conveyed. In general, the processes which are involved in the production of language tend to have more frontal locations in the brain, than the processes which are involved in the perception and comprehension of language which tend to have more posterior locations.

The Phoneme

Linguistic approaches to the study of language have emphasized the sounds in language and the grammar of language. Some linguists have argued that the brain is predisposed to analyse minimal units in the sound system of language, referred to as

phonemes. Phonemic units are contrastive. If the units differ in meaning, then the difference in sound is important. If a difference in sound is merely generated by a regional accent and does not produce a difference in meaning, then it is not important. In English there are phonemic differences between the vowels. Thus, for example, the words *slip* and *sleep* have a difference in English which produces a differing meaning. So, there are different phonemes involved in these two words. Jakobson and Halle (1956) argued that the phonemic system of every language could be characterized in terms of a small number of binary feature oppositions. They referred to these as **distinctive features** and believed that they had physical and psychological reality. They argued that the nervous system had evolved to ensure both the production and the discrimination of these features: a mere twelve basic oppositions, out of which each language made its own selections. Phonemes then can be described as sets of distinctive features. Distinguishing each phoneme from every other phoneme in the language is the presence or absence of at least one feature.

The differing features involved in four related sounds, the **stop consonants** p, b, t and d are illustrated in fig. 4.1. Whereas vowels are formed by letting the vocal chords vibrate as air moves through the mouth in an open static configuration, consonants are formed by constricting part of the mouth to complete or near

	p	b	t	d
stops	+	+	+	+
labial	+	+	−	−
alveolar	−	−	+	+
voiced	−	+	−	+

4.1 The stop consonants: These are distinguishable on the basis of the place of articulation and the presence or absence of voicing.

closure. This impedes the rush of air through the mouth and produces a distinctive sound. For the four stop consonants the flow of air is stopped by a total closure of part of the mouth. The point at which this closure occurs differs. For the sounds *p* and *b*, the closure is between the lips and these are called **labials**. For the sounds *t* and *d*, the closure or place of articulation is between the tongue and the alveolar ridge of the gums and these sounds are called **alveolar**. These points of closure are called places of articulation and are indicated in fig. 4.2. The sounds may be further distinguished by the presence or absence of **voicing**. For

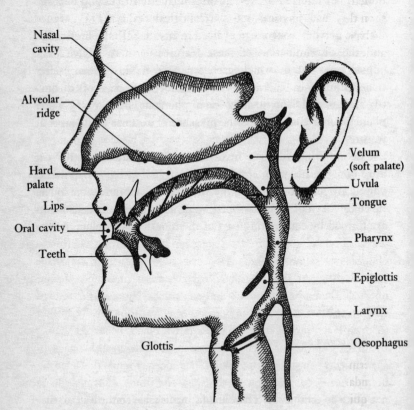

Nasal cavity

Alveolar ridge

Hard palate

Lips

Oral cavity

Teeth

Velum (soft palate)

Uvula

Tongue

Pharynx

Epiglottis

Larynx

Oesophagus

Glottis

4.2 Places of articulation.

sounds which are voiced, the closure of the vocal tract is released earlier and the vocal chords vibrate earlier. You can feel the difference which this creates in the vocal tract by placing the fingers on the throat, while attempting to make the sound *p* and the sound *b*. It should be possible to feel the vibration associated with the sound *b* earlier. Thus, the four stop consonants can be distinguished from other sounds by the total closure of the vocal tract which takes place when they are produced. They may be distinguished from each other by two features: the place of articulation and the presence or absence of voicing. Jakobson and Halle argued that the nervous system is particularly developed to focus upon the contrasts produced by these distinctive features.

Experimental support for Jakobson and Halle's hypothesis comes from studies of **categorical perception**. We have illustrated above how the sounds *b* and *p* differ mainly in the timing of voice onset. Sounds can be artificially synthesized on a computer so that there is a gradation at the moment of voice onset. When voice onset is early we know that we hear the sound *b*. When voice onset is late we know that we hear the sound *p*. Lisker and Abramson (1970) assessed what was perceived when voice onset occurred at intermediate levels between what would traditionally be considered a *b* and what would traditionally be considered a *p*. The results of this experiment are illustrated in fig. 4.3. Voice onset time was varied from − 0·15 seconds to + 0·15 seconds in steps of 0·01 of a second. This produced thirty-one distinct syllables which were presented in random order for identification. At the intermediate voice onset times, people did not hear a sound between a *p* and a *b*; rather, there was a sudden sharp transition at which the perception of a *b* dramatically shifted to the perception of a *p*. This sharp boundary occurred over a width of only about a twentieth of a second. In the series of experiments on this principle it has been found that similar boundaries occur for vowels, but the sharpness of transition is not quite as great as for consonants. It appears from these experiments that the human brain is predisposed to categorize sounds

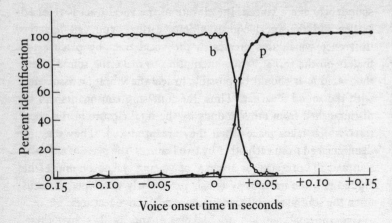

4.3 Categorical perception: A sharp border occurs between perception of the sound *b* and the sound *p*.

into one phonemic category or another. It does not simply analyse language as a continuous flow of acoustic input but imposes its own interpretation upon the signals it hears.

Cocktail Party Phenomenon

Examples of the brain's capacity to impose interpretation upon the acoustic input which it receives are shown in studies of the intelligibility of speech. Pollack and Pickett (1964) recorded spontaneous conversation without the participants' knowledge. The tape recording was then dissected into recordings of individual words. These individual word recordings were played to people who were asked to identify what they heard. Surprisingly, played in isolation, only about half of the words were intelligible. The same effects are apparent after dissecting tapes of texts being read. When the texts are read slowly, just over half of the dissected words are intelligible in isolation. When the texts are read quickly only about 40 per cent of the dissected words are identifiable. Yet, when we are listening to continuous speech, we do not have the impression that we are guessing and filling in gaps. The speech sounds clear. If the tape recordings are divided into larger and larger segments, then the intelligibility of the speech increases. The normal clarity of speech is an illusion. The brain imposes an interpretation upon the speech that it hears and constructs hypotheses about the general context and meaning, which enables the interpretation of much of the input. So, when two people claim that they heard a speaker say something slightly different, or when a person claims to have said something and their friend claims that they said something different, it may be that both are accurate. Each of them may have heard, in terms of a higher-level interpretation by the brain, a different utterance.

In normal conversational speech, the possibility of errors in speech perception are reduced by the added linguistic cues which we receive from the lip movements and facial patterning of the speaker. Difficulty in discerning and deciphering speech is of greater significance when the speech is being conveyed across telephone lines or via signals, where the speaker's face is not seen. The possibility of error is of obvious concern to the military when important messages regarding manoeuvres and actions are conveyed down pathways with reduced acoustic signals.

The perception of speech may sometimes be a rather automatic process. We may not be aware that we are monitoring conversations in which we are not taking part. At a party you may be able to identify your own name in a conversation across the room despite apparent unawareness of the content of the rest of the conversation. In order to distinguish that your name was spoken, the brain must have been monitoring the progress and acoustic pattern of the conversation which was taking place elsewhere, even though you do not notice yourself doing this. It appears that we can have the capacity to monitor more than one chain of speech at once, though it may not be possible for us to monitor both to the same degree, or for us to have full conscious awareness of the content of both.

We are also able to attend selectively to one conversation, even if there are loud competing conversations in the background, by extracting the relevant auditory information from the complex signal of intermingled speech. This is referred to as the **cocktail party phenomenon**.

When auditory speech information enters the ears it is transformed and passed on, reaching a final relay station in the **medial geniculate body** at the base of the **thalamus**, from where it travels to the primary projection area in **Heschl's gyrus**. Other areas involved in speech perception are predominantly in the temporal lobes of the brain. As you move away from the area around Heschl's gyrus into the area of the middle temporal gyrus, the region becomes more involved with the meanings associated with specific words rather than the discrimination of speech sounds *per se*. Thus, the aphasic disorders which result from damage in these areas differ from those in which there is phonological disturbance.

Language lateralization

The association of the left hemisphere of the brain with language has been known since the end of the nineteenth century. In 1861, Broca exhibited the brain of his patient 'Tan', who had died the day before and who, prior to death, had lost the power of speech so that the only word he could say was 'Tan'. The lesion included the posterior part of the left frontal lobe. Later in 1861, Broca exhibited a similar case of a patient who had lost the power of speech and the ability to write, but who could still comprehend language. Autopsy of this patient also revealed a left-hemisphere lesion. Later he went on to describe a further eight cases, but he was always cautious about his conclusions.

Here are eight cases where the lesion is situated in the posterior portion of the third frontal convolution ... and a most remarkable thing, in all these patients the lesion is on the left side. I do not dare make a conclusion. I await new findings.

Finally, in 1885, Broca published his famous dictum: 'Nous parlons avec l'hémisphère gauche.' Broca had demonstrated left-hemisphere dominance for language.

The Aphasias

Following Broca, there was a flurry of activity. In 1878, Hughlings Jackson noted that there were two types of aphasic patients, fluent and non-fluent. In 1898, Bastian argued that there were patients who had deficits, not only in the articulation of words, but also in the memory for words. Bastian postulated a visual centre for words, an auditory centre and a kinaesthetic centre for the hand and tongue. The centres were connected and information was processed in different ways by each of them. Lesions in different centres would produce different syndromes. Thus, Bastian viewed the brain as a processor.

In 1874, Carl Wernicke described a case of a patient with a **left superior temporal gyrus** lesion and this area of the brain is now often referred to as **Wernicke's area**. The patient had difficulty comprehending speech. Wernicke thought that in this posterior area of the brain there was an auditory centre for sound images, whereas Broca's area contained images for movement. These areas had to be connected by a fibre tract. This predicted that a further lesion in an intermediate area would produce a disconnection of the area for sound images from the area for images of movement leading to a difficulty in repeating words. Wernicke's scheme could account for aphasias affecting the production of language, the comprehension of language and those in which repetition was particularly impaired. A year later, Lichteim (1885) elaborated on Wernicke's ideas. He devised a complex scheme that intended to explain mechanisms underlying seven types of speech and language disorders as illustrated in Fig. 4.4. Lichteim's house contains three centres: a centre for analysing acoustic input (A) located in Wernicke's area; a centre for

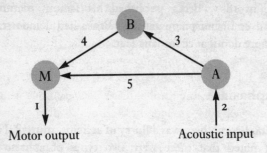

4.4 Lichteim's (1885) model of language: A – acoustic input;
B – concept centre; M – motor output.

generating motor output (M) located in Broca's area; and a
'concept centre' (B). Different aphasiological disorders could be
accounted for by lesions to different pathways or centres.

There are many different systems for classifying the aphasias
which makes reading of the aphasiological literature confusing.
However, many of the schemes contain similar disorders which
are labelled with different names. Most schemes include some
form of aphasia which particularly affects the production of language and which in many traditional schemas is referred to as
Broca's aphasia. In Lichteim's model this form of aphasia results from damage to centre M in fig. 4.4. In Broca's aphasia,
language production is not fluent and speech lacks its normal
prosodic quality. Speech resembles that used in a telegram, with
many of the grammatical words absent and only short concrete
words expressed. Thus, on my arrival to test a patient with Broca's
aphasia one day, the patient said to me, 'Nose.' From the patient's
perspective this was meant as a social communication, indicating
that she had a cold. Given the context of her language abilities,
this was an appropriate telegramatic form of the message. However, if you were not aware of her particular pattern of speech
difficulty, it would have seemed a rather unconventional communication. Patients with Broca's aphasia may vary in the severity
of their language disorder. Some are able to produce only a small

number of words, whereas others have a larger vocabulary to draw from. In Broca's aphasia, difficulties with understanding language do not mirror the language production difficulties. There can be relatively good comprehension of language. The patient may not be able to speak and express well what they are thinking but they may be able to understand any conversations which take place about them and around them. Broca's aphasics also have difficulty in repeating language. In other schemas aphasias, similar to Broca's aphasia, are sometimes referred to as **non-fluent aphasias** or **productive aphasias**. The term **motor aphasia** is also employed.

In many ways Wernicke's aphasia forms a **double dissociation** with Broca's aphasia. In Lichteim's model this form of aphasia results from damage to centre A in figure 4.4. Speech in Broca's aphasia is not fluent, whereas in Wernicke's aphasia it is very fluent, but the content of the speech may be difficult to comprehend because extra words are often introduced into the speech which are inappropriate or are new words. Thus, the Wernicke's aphasic patient may be said to use a jargon of their own and this type of language impairment is sometimes referred to as **jargon aphasia**. In other areas of speech they may substitute an incorrect word, making **paraphasic** errors which can be difficult to decipher. The following passage of speech provides an example of jargon aphasia though classical Wernicke's aphasia would have better preservation of grammar. The patient is trying to describe the accident she had falling off her horse and how her brother, a doctor, brought her to hospital. Despite the disorder in her speech it is possible to extract some of the message.

But this time, the first time, I think was the first time in years anyway, I have been fallen, been ill, and I was unconscious really, apart from the odd chap, brother who's a doctor and his son who's going to start training at Christmas er at Cambridge. Umm I gather that I talked to them alright when in fact what happened between the [jargon] and the Thursday I was, of being here I was out completely. I mean I might have come home, I mean I might have come here and talked for a couple of hours or [jargon] something or something, but in fact, I don't remember anything at all. I was completely knocked out straight . . . He's now got training them or running them on. The thing was I had fallen off an animal that became mine, that I had ridden before . . . he must have taken off that [jargon] because he wasn't one that was going to grin and stay . . . and four days apart from the odd bit that I did come through, really, taken by and large, for four days I was unconscious due to falling from him. Though I had on a horse system [jargon] that I had never experienced before but he has really found something whereas I go completely simple.

A patient with Broca's aphasia frequently has relatively good insight into their language disorder whereas patients with Wernicke's aphasia often lack this insight. They may not be aware that the pattern of their speech production is difficult to understand. Further, they have poor comprehension of language and have difficulty understanding what is being communicated to them. This pattern of language production which is difficult to understand, combined with poor comprehension and poor insight into their difficulty, may contribute to the development of psychosis in some patients with Wernicke's aphasia. It is hard for some of them to comprehend why people are not communicating with them appropriately.

Wernicke predicted that there should be connections between the systems for the production of language and the systems for the comprehension of language. This connection is marked as pathway 5 in Lichteim's model in fig. 4.4. In anatomical terms the tract is the **arcuate fasciculus**, which is important in transmission between Wernicke's area and Broca's area. Lesions affecting the area of the arcuate fasciculus result in disorders where there are particular difficulties in repetition. These disorders are referred to as **conduction aphasias**. The region of damage is in the left inferior parietal lobe. There is a severe repetition deficit. Speech is fluent but with paraphasic errors and word-finding difficulty.

In some aphasic disorders repetition is intact. These are referred to as **transcortical aphasias**, as it seems to be possible for messages to cross the cortex despite language impairment. In **transcortical motor aphasia**, resulting from destruction of pathway 4 in fig. 4.4, there is a lack of spontaneous speech and a similar pattern of speech output to Broca's aphasia. Also like Broca's aphasia there is good comprehension, but the contrast with Broca's aphasia is that repetition is intact. In **transcortical sensory aphasia**, resulting from destruction of pathway 3 in fig. 4.4, there is fluency of speech but word-finding difficulties with impaired comprehension. Thus, this pattern of aphasia resembles that of Wernicke's aphasia but is differentiated from it by the good nature of repetition.

Many patients with aphasic disorders have difficulty in retrieving words in their vocabularies. In patients for whom this characteristic is predominant, the aphasia is referred to as **anomic aphasia**. In anomic aphasia, repetition is intact, speech is fluent and comprehension is good. There are a few paraphasic errors in speech production, but there is a lack of substantive words. Thus, there is much use of the word 'thing' or 'something' or long pauses in speech, indicating that there is difficulty with word retrieval. All of us may have difficulty in finding words in our vocabulary on certain occasions; we often refer to this as the **tip-of-the-tongue-phenomenon** if the word seems near to access and we have some feeling that we know it. In patients with anomic aphasia, these normal word-finding difficulties are greatly exaggerated so that they have difficulty in retrieving words even for relatively common items. The following passage of speech illustrates the difficulty of an anomic aphasia. She is being asked to describe a picture of two children in a kitchen. One of the children is balancing on a stool trying to reach a tin of biscuits. A woman is washing dishes at the sink and the water is overflowing.

'We have two of those at home (points to the children). This one and the other one who's younger. There's one younger and one a bit *olger* ... older. One older. Yes. That one. The other one is ... there's another one. He's an entirely different person. Mmmmmm not the same as that one. One's ... one is like me (she points to the girl) and

this is not (she points to the boy). He's . . . whatever his name is . . .
I'm sorry.'

The naming difficulties of anomic aphasics are also conspicuous
when they are asked questions.

TESTER: What do we tell the time with?
ANOMIC: The time with things . . . the time things.
TESTER: What do we do with soap?
ANOMIC: We soap things . . . we soap things to make things . . .
TESTER: What do we cut paper with?
ANOMIC: We cut something . . . I'm sorry . . . It's completely . . .
TESTER: What do you do with a pencil?
ANOMIC: With a pencil should be . . . to . . . I mean I know they should
be write. I never can remember the name for it. No, it's no good.

The anomic is unable to expand upon the vocabulary of the
question in her answer. As a result she is unable to answer the
questions, though she can mime a response. In the final example
with the pencil she actually articulates an accurate response *write*
but does not recognize that she has accessed a name correctly.

Lichteim explained anomic aphasia as arising from damage to
the concept centre in fig. 4.4. However, most current theories of
anomia assume that knowledge about concepts is intact. The
patient knows what they are trying to say but there is difficulty in
accessing the appropriate verbal label. Similarly, on picture-
naming tasks, they recognize the picture and have knowledge
about the concept that is represented but cannot trigger the
object's name from this information. In current interpretations,
damage to Lichteim's concept centre would result in a different
disorder called **word-meaning deafness**, in which auditory perception for speech sounds is clear but they cannot be associated
with their meaning. Luria has suggested that in this type of
disorder, language sounds to the patient as though it consists of
words taken from a foreign language.

The anatomical areas of the brain associated with the different
types of aphasic disorder are illustrated in fig. 4.5. It is clear that

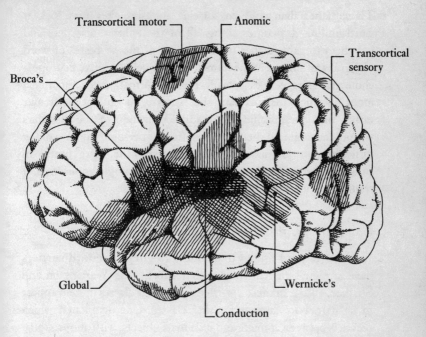

Transcortical motor — Anomic

Transcortical sensory

Broca's

Global — Wernicke's

Conduction

4.5 Anatomical areas associated with the aphasias.

certain of the aphasias appear to have more focal localization than others.

Through the twentieth century, fashions have varied regarding the validity and viability of localizing the language functions and aphasic disorders. Aphasia may show itself in a variety of forms and pure forms of the aphasic disorders described above may be rare. Many patients do not fit neatly into a Broca's, Wernicke's or anomic category. They may display some but not all of the characteristics associated with the syndrome labels. This does not mean that there are not different aphasic disorders and that these are not susceptible to some form of fractionation and division. However, many contemporary researchers of aphasia argue that rather than describing patients in terms of specific syndromes, it is better to analyse their performance in relation to specific features.

Thus, rather than studying anomic aphasics, they may look at word-finding difficulties across all of the aphasic disorders and use them to gain further understanding of the processes of word retrieval and storage in the human brain. Such cognitive neuropsychological perspectives provide more information for functional models, which may explain the patterns of patient behaviour rather than the specific anatomical localization of the disorders within the brain. A better conceptual understanding of naming difficulties or grammatical difficulties may be more useful in constructing theory-driven therapy than the simple application of traditional syndrome labels.

Category-specific Disorders

In studies of word-finding difficulties **category-specific disorders** have attracted current interest and debate (e.g. Warrington and Shallice, 1984). In these disorders, particular classes of item appear to be harder to name than other classes. One distinction which recurs is between animate and inanimate objects, with one grouping sometimes being selectively impaired whilst the other is selectively preserved. So there are some patients who can name scissors and a microscope but cannot name a horse. It could be argued that this suggests there are different categories in the brain for animate and inanimate objects, which are coded in different locations, but the basis for this distinction is unclear. Is there something different about the way in which animate and inanimate objects are encoded which causes them to be stored in a differing way, or is there something different about the way they are retrieved? One hypothesis is that animate objects are more often associated with sensory features relevant to their appearance, whereas inanimate objects are often associated with particular functional uses. Others have argued that animate objects tend to be more visually complex than inanimate ones and also resemble each other more. Thus, for example, a zebra, a horse, a camel and a lion are all of approximately similar size and have four legs, a tail and a neck. It is specific sensory features which enable us to distinguish between them. When referring to objects which are found in a house, like a ruler, scissors, bed or telephone, an integral part of our knowledge about these objects often relates to the specific function which they have in our life or the way in which we use them. Such theories would suggest a different form of aphasic disorder to be found amongst gamekeepers, zoo keepers or vets than amongst the rest of the population, since animals play a different role in the lives of these people.

The most selective category-specific deficit has been reported by Hart, Berndt and Caramazza (1985) who described an impairment of naming fruit and vegetables with preservation of the naming of other foods, animals, body parts, clothes, shapes, trees and household objects. The patient, who was unable to name a *peach* and an *orange*, could name correctly an *abacus* and the verb *thinks*. The deficit was specific to naming things presented in a visual modality as the patient could point to fruit and vegetables named verbally and could categorize their written names. In interpreting modality-specific deficits, some researchers argue that there is a single semantic system which stores the meaning of words and their names, but there are a variety of access routes to and from this store which may be differentially affected. Hart *et al* suggested that their patient showed impairment within the name-retrieval routes. Other researchers believe that there are several modality-specific semantic systems, and that the store of meaning which is accessed in one task is not the same as the store of meaning which is accessed in another.

Although category-specific deficits have now been extensively documented, it is more common to see anomic effects extending across categories, but being affected by the frequency of the word which is being activated. All of us are more rapid at accessing common words in our vocabulary than rare and unusual words. In many patients with word-finding difficulties, this effect is greatly exaggerated, so that words of even moderate frequency in a vocabulary are difficult to access. The patient may show understanding of the word they are trying to find by producing a description which goes around the word; this is referred to as a **circumlocution**. Thus, for example, in trying to retrieve the word racetrack the patient may say, 'Horses . . . running . . . money . . . win . . . people . . . sunny.'

The Role of the Right Hemisphere

We have stressed the role of the left hemisphere of the brain in language. However, it would be a mistake to imply that, when communicating with language, the right hemisphere is inactive. Indeed, blood-flow studies indicate that during language processing there is considerable blood flow to the right hemisphere. We also know that damage to the right hemisphere of the brain does not produce the dramatic impairments of language which can be produced by damage to the left. This raises the question of the role of the right hemisphere in language processing. A number of different language functions have been postulated. It has been suggested that the humorous elements of language, for example, the ability to perceive wit and innuendo, are part of the right hemisphere's role. It is also able to make non-literal interpretations of language which may be important in the comprehension of sarcasm and metaphor. Patients with right-hemisphere damage tend to make more literal interpretations of language and display subtle disorders of communication. It has also been suggested that the right hemisphere may play a crucial role in providing the appropriate emotional intonation contours to language. Patients with right-hemisphere damage are sometimes described as having rather flat, uninteresting speech. The right hemisphere may also aid in providing the general environment in which the language is to be uttered. It may contribute to the selection of specific items from within the vocabulary and provide a context for the communications. In many people, the right hemisphere may have some basic vocabulary skills which overlap with the left hemisphere, but it seems that the right hemisphere has only very basic grammatical skills. It is not able to deal with the complexities of syntax analysis necessary for normal speech production and comprehension. It also has difficulty with sound-based phonological elements of language and in the processing of rhyme.

Left Handers

The distinctions which have been drawn between the right and left hemisphere are probably valid for the majority of right-handed people. Evidence from a variety of studies of both brain-damaged and normal people would suggest that about 98 per cent of right handers have left-hemisphere lateralization for language. However, the picture for left handers is less clear cut. Annett (1985) has argued that there is a genetic factor which increases the possiblity of the left hemisphere subserving speech. An incidental effect of this is to shift the distribution of hand differences and skill towards a right-hemisphere superiority. This **right-shift factor** is carried on a single allele. The alternative allele is uncommitted for speech and, hence, handedness. This means that an increased probability of right-handedness is genetically programmed but left-handedness is not. Annett's model is illustrated in fig. 4.6. This indicates that if one looks at the distribution of skills between the right and the left hand, the distribution is composed of two different distributions which are overlapping. For individuals who have a right-shift factor, labelled RS+ in fig. 4.6, the mean of the distribution is to the right-hand end of the scale. Most of these people will be right-handed and only a very small number left-handed. The second distribution is made up of those individuals who lack the right shift factor, labelled RS− in fig. 4.6. For these individuals, it will be a random event whether they are right-handed or left-handed; the mean of the distribution is at a point where there is no superiority of skill with one or other hand. Half of the people in this distribution will be left-handed. Thus the population of left handers will be made up largely from people who lack a right-shift factor and with some who have a right-shift factor.

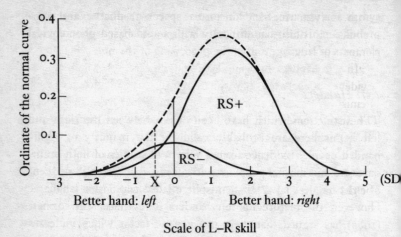

4.6 The right shift theory: The distribution of skills between the right and left hand is composed of two overlapping distributions from those with the shift factor (RS +), and those without (RS −).

Thus, many left handers will lack the factor which predisposes the left hemisphere to subserve speech.

Studies by Milner (1974) in Canada suggest that in left handers or ambidextrous individuals, in whom there is no evidence of left-hemisphere damage, approximately 70 per cent will have left-hemisphere speech representation. The rest of the left handers will have either right-hemisphere speech representations or bilateral speech representations. It is not the case that left handers are simply like right handers in mirror image. They show a bias towards superiority in hand use which is the opposite of that of right handers, but their brains are not simply the opposite of those of right handers. A further complicating factor in understanding left-handedness is that left handers are in general not as strongly left-handed as right handers are right-handed. Many left handers still do some things with their right hands. Further, many studies divide left handers into those in whom there is a familial history of sinistrality and those in whom there is none.

Both strength in handedness and the presence or absence of familial sinistrality appear to relate to underlying differences in brain organization.

In left handers or amibidextrous subjects, for whom there is evidence of early left-hemisphere damage, the incidence of right-hemisphere speech representation is higher at over 50 per cent. These left handers may originally have been predisposed to develop language in the left hemisphere but it may have shifted because of the early left-hemisphere damage. Such left handers are sometimes referred to as **pathological left handers**. It may be the presence of them in any left-handed population which may contribute to the higher incidence of left-handedness found in association with a variety of disorders. However, left-handedness is also associated with particular skills. Amongst populations and occupations which are dependent upon superior skills in applied spatial areas and areas requiring three-dimensional visualization there is an elevated incidence of left-handedness. Such areas would include certain areas of sport and areas of mathematics and engineering. So left handers differ from right handers in their brain organization, and among left handers there are also individual differences. The distribution and organization of language is one of the areas in which left handers differ from right handers.

Animal Language

The capacity of the human brain to process language is sometimes seen as what distinguishes us from other members of the animal kingdom. Although other animals use communication systems and some of these are relatively sophisticated, no other animal communication system is capable of the range and complexity of messages which human language enables. Many animal species are able to communicate a fixed number of messages about specific topics or a variable number of messages about specific topics. Attempts to teach chimps and apes gestural communication systems, to show that man's capacity for language is not unique, met with initial apparent success, but subsequent scepticism. Overall, these studies have indicated that it is possible for other species to develop a large range of vocabulary items which they may attempt to use to some extent in a communicative context, but they are unable to learn an appropriate grammatical system for combining these elements. In many cases, their use of the communication system is directly prompted by the humans with whom they interact. Humans with their language system are able to use a restricted number of elements in combination to produce a potentially infinite number of utterances. This flexibility in their communication system and the brain's great talent for acquiring the system and utilizing it have significantly contributed to human advancement. The brains of animals are not predisposed to acquire a comparable skill.

Learning Grammar

Children are not explicitly taught language, in the sense that they are not corrected whenever they make an error and do not have specific grammatical rules pointed out to them. It is possible to learn a second language in a formal way via explicit instruction, but children will naturally acquire language if they are exposed to it. For some children there may be particular difficulty in acquiring language at its normal rate or there may be components which are difficult to acquire but for the majority of humans it is something which develops spontaneously. In the attempts to teach animals language they were able to teach a number of words if these were attached to signs or symbols but there was no evidence of grammatical mastery. A child's mastery of grammatical rules is central to its language acquisition.

In the heyday of behaviourism in the fifties and sixties, it had been believed that learning theory could account for language development. Much of learning theory was based on the principles of Skinner, who argued that when behaviour was rewarded it would occur with greater frequency. A speaker's performance was considered to be based on probability counts of a finite number of sentences that the speaker had heard before. However, this account of language does not explain the potentially infinite number of grammatical sentences which we may produce. Also, the process of acquiring stimulus-response probabilities would be very uneconomical. Following behaviourism, linguists attempted to analyse the grammar of language in order to produce a description of its basic structure. In these endeavours Chomsky played a crucial role. He argued that man had an innate **language acquisition device** and that this biologically inherited mechanism was common to all humans. The process of the grammatical decomposition of language was seen, therefore, as biologically driven by a genetically programmed neural substrate in the brain.

Prior to Chomsky's work, there existed a number of **phrase structure grammars**. These consisted of many rewrite rules, which enabled the rewriting of sentences in progressively smaller units. Thus, for example, a sentence could be rewritten as a noun phrase plus a verb phrase. The verb phrase could be rewritten as a verb plus a noun phrase. A noun phrase might be rewritten as an article and a noun (see fig. 4.7). These phrase structure grammars represent a structural description of sentences. However, they did not give the order in which the rules had to be applied and correct ordering can be a problem in writing complex grammar for a range of sentences, for example, to deal with embedded clauses. Chomsky introduced a **transformational grammar**, which aimed to be able to describe all the sentences which were valid sentences in a language and would produce no sentences that were invalid sentences in a language. There were two early versions of Chomsky's theory. His 1957 grammar consisted of three types of rules. **Phrase structure rules** were rewrite rules which produced strings which could be represented by hierarchical tree diagrams and resembled the phrase structure grammars mentioned above. **Transformational rules** operated on the

Jane likes the dog

1. S → NP + VP
3. NP → N
4. VP → V + NP
2. NP → art + N
7. N → Jane
8. V → likes
10. art → the
7. N → dog

4.7 A phrase structure tree.

overall structures of phrase structure strings, so as to produce the strings underlying sentences in their final form. In other words, transformational rules were more complicated rules about the way in which bits of phrases related to each other and could be shifted from one position to another. **Morphophonemic rules** converted the strings that were generated by these rules into the actual sounds of a sentence and were responsible for the phonological output.

Transformational rules were of two sorts. They were either **obligatory** or **optional**. Obligatory rules are responsible, for example, for the agreement between a noun and its verb. Thus, for example, the verb 'win' must take an 's' if it is in the singular form. If at the races, you are placing a bet, you hope that *your horse wins* with an 's'. However, if you are unlucky and several horses cross the line together requiring a photo-finish analysis, it may be that *the horses win*, without an 's', and you have to divide your winnings. Thus, in Chomsky's terms, obligatory transformations are those which are necessary for a sentence to be grammatically correct. In addition, there are optional transformations which may alter the meaning of a sentence. If you are unlucky at the races, you may find that instead of *the horse wins*, the appropriate sentence is *the horse does not win*. Negatives are processed by optional rules. Further, if you are in the bar having a drink when the horses crossed the racing line and you do not see which wins, you may be required to ask 'Did the horse win?' Questions are also controlled by optional rules.

In 1965, Chomsky modified his theory. The original theory had been criticized because it took no account of the meaning of words. It could generate sentences which were grammatically correct, but which did not make sense. The much-quoted sentence 'Colourless green ideas sleep furiously' conforms to the principles of Chomsky's 1957 theory, but does not conform to the principles of an appropriate sentence in English since it is meaningless. In 1965, Chomsky basically introduced meanings or **semantics** into his theory, which now had three components. It had a **syntactic component** which consisted of the phrase-structure rules of the earlier theory, which were now called **base rules**, and also the transformational rules of the earlier theory. These rules differed a little from the earlier version, since there were further constraints regarding individual words, that is, the **lexicon** was introduced.

Besides the syntactic component there was also a **phonological component**, which replaced the morphophonemic rules of the earlier theory, and, finally, a **semantic component** was introduced. In this version of the theory, account was taken of the fact that certain types of agents can only perform certain types of actions. So, if using a verb like *galloped*, the subject is animate and of a specific type like *horse*. In the 1965 version of this theory, Chomsky also introduced the notions of **deep structure** and **surface structure**. The utterance which is produced contains the surface structure. Underlying this are basic messages which comprise the deep structure. Transformations convert the deep structure into the surface structure. In this later version of the theory, things like passives and negatives are marked in the deep structure. Thus, all transformations are obligatory and none are optional. It is the deep structure which is the basis of the semantic interpretation and the meaning of what is conveyed. '*The racing of the horses is awful*' is ambiguous because it has two deep structures. The deep structure brings out the underlying grammatical relationship in the sentence. Chomsky argued that an innate language-acquisition device made all children's brains develop in such a way that they have a predisposition to develop this one universal type of grammar.

If a child is deprived of linguistic input throughout the early childhood years, then language does not develop normally. An example of such a case is the child, Genie, who has been studied by Fromkin *et al* (1974). Genie was kept, from an early age, locked up in a room away from human and language contact. She may have had some minimal exposure to written verbal information, because when she was found she was able to turn pages with her foot, suggesting that she may have had in the room with her some magazines or papers. However, she had had no sustained verbal input and when she was found as a teenager she could neither read nor write. Attempts have been made since this time to teach her language. Genie has been able to acquire a communication system but there has been a severe restriction in the nature of linguistic development which has been possible. She has had much greater difficulty in acquiring the grammar of language than in acquiring specific vocabulary items. There is also evidence that her language has not developed in the normal left-hemispheric system, but is developing in the right hemisphere. This suggests that there may be a critical period in the left hemisphere for the acquisition of language, beyond which its capacity to develop these skills degrades. Only in highly abnormal social situations will there be a risk that this critical period is past. The critical period may explain why languages learnt or to which a child is exposed, before a certain age, can subsequently be learnt without accent; but languages acquired after the teenage years nearly always retain a foreign accent. This critical period may be important for a language-acquisition device within the left hemisphere of the brain.

Chapter Five :
Memory and the Brain

Semantic and Episodic Knowledge

Memory enables us to make sense of the world by linking current experience with our previous knowledge about the world and how it works. We remember what words mean and what objects are. We know, at least if Scottish, that *Hogmanay* is the last day of the year and that *whisky* is a golden-coloured alcoholic beverage. This **semantic knowledge** is differentiated from personal auto-biographical knowledge, in which one may recall a particular evening of frivolity when whisky was drunk. Such **episodic knowledge** is thought to form a distinct memory system in the brain from semantic knowledge. Sometimes episodic knowledge appears to be poor, as when people fail to recall events in evenings when a lot of whisky was drunk. The biochemical effects of the alcohol interfere with the normal processes of establishing memory in the brain. The memory is either encoded ineffectively in the brain or stored correctly but its position poorly marked so that it cannot be found again. Thus, the problem is in either *storage* or *retrieval*. Those who argue that the problem is in retrieval rather than storage note that sometimes, when drunk subsequently, events associated with the previous drunkenness are recalled with alarming clarity. This effect has been called **state-dependent retrieval** and is a popular topic of research amongst university undergraduates.

Alcoholism and Amnesia

More serious memory impairments are associated with long-term alcohol abuse. When people consume large quantities of alcohol they are also consuming large quantities of calories. There is a tendency for them to neglect other areas of their diet. Since alcohol washes many vitamins out of the body the drinker should really be eating more than other people to retain comparable vitamin levels. It appears that deficiencies of thiamine, a form of Vitamin B, are particularly damaging amongst alcoholics. In the acute stage, the alcoholic has difficulty with balance and movement, is confused about both time and place, and experiences a variety of peripheral neuropathologies such as pain or loss of sensation in the extremities of limbs. These are treated with large doses of thiamine and over one or two months the difficulties with movement and sensation recede. However, the patient is left with both personality alterations and an irreversible impairment of memory called **Korsakoff amnesia**. Korsakoff patients are sometimes referred to as **diencephalic** because of the location of the lesion in their brains. Damage is thought to involve two small structures in the middle of the brain called the **mammillary bodies** and the **dorsomedial thalamus** (see fig. 5.1). There is debate about whether or not one or other of these structures is more crucial in the aetiology of their memory impairment.

Memory and Intelligence

People with very bad memories usually perform poorly on most formal scholastic examinations, whilst people with very good memories tend to perform well on such tasks. Furthermore, a good memory is often taken as a sign of good intellectual ability. However, despite their severe memory problems, the amnesic patients will perform quite adequately on tests of intellectual

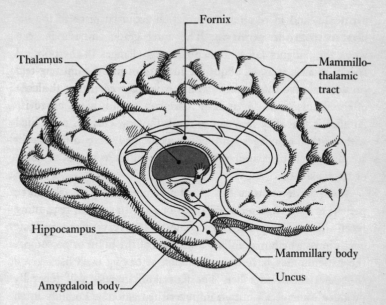

Fornix

Thalamus

Mammillo-thalamic tract

Hippocampus

Mammillary body

Uncus

Amygdaloid body

5.1 The mammillary bodies and the dorsomedial thalamus.

function. They have normal IQ scores. On a typical intelligence battery such as the Weschler, they perform normally on tests of verbal reasoning, comprehension and vocabulary and on non-verbal tasks of spatial, manipulative and constructive skill. Thus, memory and intelligence are not necessarily correlated.

In addition to normal intelligence, most amnesics have adequate social skills and normal language, therefore, on first encounter, their deficits may not be instantly apparent.

Anterograde Amnesia

The term amnesia is used to cover memory impairments in which both semantic and episodic knowledge of the world is affected. In common with most other amnesics, the Korsakoff amnesics have difficulty both in acquiring new information, **anterograde**

amnesia, and in recalling information acquired prior to the illness, **retrograde amnesia**. The anterograde amnesia is seen
when the patients fail to remember new changes in the political
spectrum and, if asked about the identity of prime ministers and
presidents, give those which would have been correct at the time
of the illness itself. What is of more concern to their immediate
families is that they may fail to recall the new changes associated
with births, marriages and deaths and may have difficulty in
adapting their behaviour if they fail to recall new moves of home
or circumstance.

Anterograde amnesia can also be demonstrated by asking the
patient to listen to a series of words or stories and then requesting
recall after a short delay. In some of the very severe amnesic
conditions, which may follow infections of the brain or poisoning,
the patients may have no recollection of having even been given
the material to remember. The Korsakoff amnesic will generally
produce some recall but an impoverished amount. Possibly in an
attempt to hide their memory impairments, when amnesics are
asked factual questions which they cannot answer, they will often
fill in with logically possible but untrue information. This is
referred to as **confabulation**. If you are not familiar with an
amnesic's day-to-day life, their confabulated descriptions can be
most convincing.

A lot of discussion in relation to Korsakoff amnesia has been
concerned with whether the problem is one of registration, storage
or retrieval. Are the memories laid down incorrectly? Is there
some failure to fix the memories in storage? Are the memories
there but cannot be found? Several sources of evidence suggest
that the memories have not completely disappeared. Sometimes
recollections are patchy and information which cannot be recalled
on one occasion is suddenly remembered on another, thus, the
memory must still have existed even when it could not be recalled.
Amnesics also make errors, called **intrusion errors**, in remembering lists of words. Typically the amnesic is given several lists of
words to remember. At the end of each list they are asked to say

all the items that they can remember. Words which were forgotten when trying to remember the earlier lists of words, are given as responses incorrectly when remembering later lists. Thus items from earlier lists which appeared to have been forgotten intrude upon the recollection of later lists. A final source of evidence that memories have been stored is the effectiveness of cues. Although performance remains poor, most amnesics do improve upon what they can remember if they are given a relevant cue or clue. This suggests that the memory is stored but their method of finding it does not work well.

Theorists who are unconvinced that amnesia is simply the result of a retrieval deficit point out that all normal performance is also helped by cues, and that the dramatic effects sometimes seen using cues with amnesics may simply result from the fact that their performance is so poor in the first place that they have much further to improve. In order to argue that there is something unusual about the retrieval abilities of amnesics, it has to be shown that cues are more effective for amnesics than for normal subjects even when their original level of performance is comparable. Such experiments can be done by comparing the patterns of memory performance of amnesics who are asked to remember material only a few minutes after they have been given it with the performance of normal subjects who have had much longer delays since they were given the material to remember. To equate initial memory levels the normal subjects may have to be tested after delays of several weeks. The conclusion of these experiments seems to be that there is no evidence that cues help amnesics any more than they help normal people.

Retrograde Amnesia

Retrograde amnesia for events prior to illness is not of equal severity for all events. Typically, it stretches back in time for a period of years before the patient's illness, but leaves childhood memories intact. Memory is worst for events just before the illness and then gets systematically better as you go back in time. This confirms what is called **Ribot's Law**: new perishes before old.

Retrograde amnesia has been most extensively studied in patients with Korsakoff amnesia. Squires (1982a) suggested that the memory gradient in these patients was misleading. Possibly the excessive alcohol intake had systematically produced poorer and poorer encoding of memories over time, with maximal effect just prior to illness. The retrograde amnesia would not then be a true memory failure for events prior to illness but would reflect the poverty with which these memories had originally been encoded. This is called the **continuity hypothesis**.

One piece of evidence against this view comes from patients with **transient global amnesia** (TGA). In this poorly understood condition, an apparently normal person will suddenly enter a state of severe amnesia, lasting from a few minutes to a few hours. Historically this has been a difficult condition to study, since by the time the researcher gets to the scene of the amnesia, the patient has usually recovered. While studying the disorder in the Oxford area, Hodges established a hotline, in response to which he would drop everything and rush to the patient's home. He managed to capture episodes of TGA on video tape and conducted some systematic testing of the patients (Hodges and Ward, 1989). The transient-global-amnesic patients also display a retrograde amnesia which conforms to Ribot's law, with a systematic gradient of memory failure affecting new memories more than old. At the time when these patients' old memories were being laid down they were not consuming excessive quantities of alcohol and did not have current memory problems. Furthermore, when their transient global amnesia passed, their recall for past events did not retain the gradient pattern. There appears to be nothing wrong with the stores for past events in these patients. They are merely temporarily and differentially unavailable.

These TGA results support an **acute onset hypothesis**. This hypothesis is also supported by Parkin *et al*'s (1991) report of a temporal gradient to the retrograde amnesia exhibited by a patient whose amnesia had sudden onset following intestinal surgery and intravenous feeding. Another case of acute onset amnesia with retrograde temporal gradient is *P.Z.*, an academic scientist who two years prior to the onset of Korsakoff syndrome had written a detailed autobiography, indicating that at this time his memory for past events through the decades was good (Butters, 1984).

Diencephalic and Hippocampal Amnesias

In addition to the Korsakoff patients, an individual case of diencephalic memory impairment has been studied extensively. *N.A.* has been severely amnesic for verbal material since 1960 when he sustained a stab wound to the brain with a miniature fencing foil. The foil damaged the left dorsomedial thalamus, one of the diencephalic areas implicated in Korsakoff syndrome. *N.A.*'s intellectual level is above average and he has no noticeable cognitive impairments other than his amnesia. His memory impairment is an anterograde amnesia, with only minimal retrograde loss (Squires and Slater, 1978).

The most studied individual in memory literature is *H.M.* (Scoville and Milner, 1957). Here the pathology is different. *H.M.* suffered from severe epilepsy which was uncontrollable even with medication. In an attempt to relieve the disorder, *H.M.* underwent a **bilateral medial temporal lobectomy**, where the inner portions of the temporal lobes were surgically removed on both sides of the brain. Several midbrain structures lying below the temporal lobes were also removed: the **uncus**, the **amygdala** and the **hippocampus**. The bilateral removal of the hippocampus is believed to be most crucial. *H.M.* has been extensively studied by Milner and her colleagues in Montreal. He has both anterograde and retrograde amnesia, though the latter has recovered to some extent, and covers only a short period of years. *H. M.* can read and reread books and articles with no recollection of having seen them before. He is continually reintroduced to the doctors who work with him as he does not remember meeting them before. To some extent he lives in a time warp. *H. M.* himself says, 'Every day is alone in itself, whatever enjoyment I've had and whatever sorrow I've had' (Milner, Corkin and Teuber, 1968).

Another group of patients with memory impairments may also have hippocampal damage. These patients have had bilateral **electroconvulsive therapy** (ECT). This is sometimes used for the relief of chronic depression, for which it seems to be moderately effective. It has also been used on individuals with other psychiatric impairments, but it is less effective for these. The treatment involves placing electrodes on either side of the head and transmitting a sufficient electrical current to induce a convulsion. Unfortunately, once the brain has sustained one seizure it is much more probable that another will occur spontaneously. Thus, one side-effect of ECT can be the development of epilepsy in which seizures occur repeatedly. Another side-effect is memory impairment. ECT patients have a temporary memory impairment which conforms to Ribot's law. Their retrograde amnesia is most profound for recent events and memory for earlier events can be intact. Squires and Cohen (1982) illustrated this in a study of the recall of television programmes which had only been screened for one season. After ECT the subjects had difficulty in remembering recent titles (see fig. 5.2). There is also an anterograde amnesia following ECT, with difficulty in recalling stories and in learning pairings of words in **paired associate** tasks. The effects of the ECT treatment upon memory recede as time passes and the extent of permanent deficits is unclear.

Some researchers think that the characteristics of the memory impairment in diencephalic amnesics differs from those with hippocampal abnormalities. In particular, it has been suggested that the diencephalic amnesics have abnormal encoding of memories

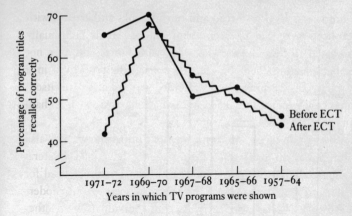

5.2 Retrograde amnesia following ECT (Squires and Cohen, 1982).

but then show normal rates of forgetting, whilst the hippocampal amnesics forget very rapidly, showing failure in the *consolidation* and *elaboration* of memories.

Addition Memory Deficits in Korsakoff Amnesia

Korsakoff patients show addition deficits which differentiate them. Craik and Lockhart (1972) proposed a theory of **levels of processing**. This said that the deeper the processing of material the better it would be remembered. Thus, if normal people have to make judgements about the **orthographic** characteristics of words their later memory for these words is poorer than the memory of those who were given a task which required focus upon the sound, rhyme or **phonological** aspects of the words (see fig. 5.3). These people were, in turn, poorer at remembering than those who actually had to look at the meaning of the words by making a **semantic** decision about them. This effect had been called the **semantic encoding effect**. In some amnesics this semantic encoding effect has also been found. Thus, although their performance is very poor they remember more if they have

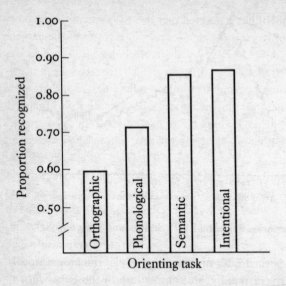

5.3 Levels of processing: Words which have been semantically encoded are remembered better than those which have been phonologically encoded and these in turn are recalled better than those which have been orthographically encoded.

been focusing on a semantic processing level rather than something more peripheral to the word. Korsakoff patients do not show this effect.

Another characteristic of normal memory is what is called **proactive interference**. If a person is required to learn a number of lists of words of similar types of material, recall in the later lists is disrupted by remembering material from earlier lists. These errors from the earlier lists have been mentioned before and are called intrusion errors. However, if the nature of the material is changed, the memory performance improves, and intrusion errors disappear. Thus, if asked to recall the names of list after list of authors, performance will improve if a list of politicians is suddenly given. This effect is called **release** from proactive interference. Korsakoff amnesics do not show this release.

Squires (1982b) has suggested that these aspects of the memory performance of Korsakoff amnesics may be a result of the damage to the frontal lobes caused by their alcohol abuse. In Chapter Two, we referred to the difficulty which frontal lobe patients have in changing set and that they exhibit inertia and rigidity, leading to difficulty in changing strategy. Release from proactive interference is dependent upon a change of set from one semantic category to another. Frontal lobe patients often show failure of release comparable to the Korsakoff amnesics. These elements of memory abnormality in the Korsakoff patients may be seen as reflecting the influence of higher level reasoning skills upon memory. Warrington and Weiskrantz (1982) distinguish between **semantic memory systems**, believed to be subserved by structures in the temporal lobes, and **mediational systems**, in which frontal structures are crucially involved. The amnesics with frontal lobe impairments are unable to store the benefits of their cognitive mediation: imagery, organization and cognitive elaboration.

What Amnesics Can Remember

It is not the case that amnesics are unable to learn anything. They show significant improvements across trials in learning new skills (Brooks and Baddeley, 1976) like tracing designs seen in a mirror (see fig. 5.4), or assembling a jigsaw. They also display classical conditioning learning and will avoid situations which have been paired previously with unpleasant events. They do this without apparent recollection of the unpleasant events themselves. This failure to remember the situation in which learning took place is consistent across the tasks. Gardner (1977) taught an amnesic a melody on the piano and found that the melody was remembered. This happened even though the amnesic did not remember the learning sessions at all.

To explain these residual memory skills a distinction has been

5.4 Mirror drawing: A form of learning
preserved in amnesia.

drawn between **procedural knowledge** and **declarative knowledge**. Procedural knowledge involves the modification of a schema or way of interpreting the world. Procedural learning is possible in amnesics since they can learn to change their response to the environment. However, amnesics cannot remember declarative knowledge. They do not remember the specific instances in which learning took place or specific factual information. One suggestion is that procedural learning may be phylogenetically more primitive. Inevitably following this distinction, there have been arguments in relation to some tasks whose categorization as either procedural or declarative is ambiguous. A more recent distinction has been drawn between tasks in which the specific occasion of learning is important in recall and those for which remembering learning itself is irrelevant.

Categories of Memory

As discussed in Chapter Two, the left cerebral hemisphere of the brain seems to be more specialized than the right for processing verbal material. Comparable asymmetries of memory have been reported by Milner (1980) in Montreal. She studied groups of patients who had undergone surgery for the treatment of epilepsy.

When a person has an epileptic seizure, the normal electrical activity of the brain is disrupted. Many millions of brain cells synchronize and fire in unison, producing a large burst of electricity which spreads across the brain. It is followed by further electrical waves. Most people with epilepsy have their seizures well controlled with drugs, but for some people drugs do not work. Amongst those not helped by drugs are a few of the people who have a **focus** to their epileptic seizures. The seizures start at the focus, and spread out from this point through the brain. The most common area for an epileptic focus to occur is in the temporal lobes, which sit over the hippocampus, therefore the temporal lobes and the hippocampus are said to be the most **epileptogenic areas** of the brain. They are also the areas of the brain thought to be crucial for memory. This association may not be random. There may be something about the electrical neural pattern of connectivity of these areas which makes them modifiable in a way useful for encoding or retrieving memories but also makes them more vulnerable to abnormality. It has been found that if a patient has severe focal epilepsy, surgically removing the area of the brain which is the focus may significantly reduce the seizure disorder. It is for this reason that there are a number of patients with epilepsy who have had a temporal lobectomy, involving the removal of the anterior temporal neocortex, the amygdala, uncus, hippocampus and parahippocampal gyrus. These are the patients whose memories have been studied by Milner.

The dramatic effects of bilateral removal of the hippocampus have been documented in the patient *H. M.* (Scoville and Milner, 1957), who was discussed earlier. The temporal lobectomy patients have had tissue removed from only one side of the brain. These unilateral operations are much less devastating in their consequences. Memory impairments follow but these depend upon the type of material which is to be remembered. Patients who have had a left temporal lobectomy have difficulty remembering passages of prose and learning new associations between pairs of words. In contrast, patients who have had a right temporal lobectomy have difficulty in remembering unfamiliar geometrical figures, nonsense figures, faces, visual and tactual mazes and musical tone sequences. The right temporal lobectomies have no difficulty in remembering verbal material. These laterality effects are consistent with other sources of information about functional lateralization in the human brain.

Some researchers have reported even more specific memory impairments depending upon the type of material that is to be remembered. These more specific deficits are seen in a variety of other types of neurological patients. Within the non-verbal sphere, De Renzi, Faglioni and Villa (1977) reported a patient who had difficulty in learning routes and mazes. This impairment of topographical memory occurred despite intact memory for other non-verbal information like faces or positions. Whiteley and Warrington (1977) describe a dissociation in memory for complex visual objects. Their patients had poor memory for the names of famous buildings but had good memory for the names of famous faces.

A variety of other **category specific** deficits have been reported by Warrington and various co-workers (for example, Warrington and Shallice, 1984). They find dissociations between a variety of semantic categories. One of the more common dissociations seems to be between animals and household objects. Thus some patients will show selective difficulty with one or other group. It is argued that these differences reflect a categorical organization to the semantic memory system itself. What remains unresolved is whether the storage system has box-like categories or whether there is something about the material in certain categories which makes it susceptible to encoding or reactivating in particular ways.

Animals may be more commonly differentiated in terms of their appearance and particular visual features, for example, zebras have stripes; giraffes have long necks. In contrast household objects may be closely associated with a particular function, for example, hammers are used for pounding nails; rulers are used for drawing lines. Humphreys and Riddoch (1987) have argued that it is not just that animals are more commonly differentiated on the basis of their visual features but animals and certain other categories consist of sets of items which are visually fairly similar. They think that the visual distinctiveness of one category member to another is a significant variable. Currently we know that a variety of category specific disorders exist but a consensus has not been reached of the best theoretical account for them, in relation to semantic memory systems.

Boxers

A common cause of memory impairment is **closed head injury**. When the head receives an external blow it is usually cushioned by the fluid which sits between the brain and the skull. If you hit your head suddenly on a cupboard door or low doorway you are most unlikely to have any resulting memory problems. However, if you receive a severe blow in a traffic accident or fight which is sufficient to produce loss of consciousness, then memory may be affected. The blows appear to cause shearing of brain tissue and some of the midbrain structures involved in memory may be particularly vulnerable to this effect. On regaining consciousness, there is commonly a retrograde amnesia for events prior to the injury. As a rough guide, the shorter the period of loss of consciousness and the shorter the retrograde amnesia, the more probable the retention of good memory skills.

Boxers receive repeated blows to the head over periods of many years. Severe memory impairments are common amongst former professional boxers. The British Medical Association has voiced its concern over the sport and professional boxers are now required to have regular brain scans. Unfortunately, by the time abnormality is visible on a brain scan, the damage is done and the consequences for memory are irreversible.

Memory and Old Age

As we get older we are often aware that our memories seem to be getting poorer. Day to day, there seems to be increasing difficulty in remembering where things have been put and which things have to be remembered to be done. There are complaints of absentmindedness. The episodic autobiographical component of memory appears to be more affected than factual semantic memory. One theory about poor memory in old age is that there is a **production deficiency** which results from poor organization of the material which has to be learnt. There is some evidence that old people have greater difficulty remembering material which they have to organize themselves than highly structured and pre-organized material. An alternative theory is that old people have difficulty in remembering peripheral information (Rabbitt, 1982). Information which does not seem directly relevant to the material being learnt is noted less, which may make the subsequent memory accessible from fewer cues. This type of theory implies that older people have reduced processing resources to use in memory tasks.

Most older and elderly people retain sufficient memory capacities to enable them to conduct their life normally. They work to retirement age, pursue leisure interests, travel, socialize and continually learn new information about the world in which they are living. They keep track of political developments, current affairs and new innovations, and also the changing activities and lives of their families, friends and neighbours. Unfortunately, a minority of old people experience a more rapid decline in both their intellectual processes and their memories. This process used to be differentiated into senile and pre-senile **dementia**, dependent upon the age at onset of the symptoms. There is now little evidence that the two are distinct conditions and the term dementia tends to be employed without reference to age.

Dementia

The most common cause of the dementias is **Alzheimer's disease**. This diagnosis is reached where the symptoms of dementia have no other clear cause. However, the diagnosis is only definitive at post-mortem, when the brain is found to contain numerous **neurofibrillary tangles and plaques**. The latter contain deposits of amyloid protein. Throughout the brain, groupings of neurons are stuck together or tangled up. The precise cause of Alzheimer's disease is not known. Attention has focussed on the high levels of aluminium in the brains at post-mortem. Some metabolic abnormality could be producing these concentrations. If environmental exposure to aluminium is at root, its source is unclear. Whilst there has been media attention on possible sources, from a scientific perspective these remain highly speculative.

If environmental exposure is relevant, it is almost certainly not the only precipitating factor. Dementia is frequently noticed to be more common in some families than in others, and in families with early onset (< 65 years) of Alzheimer's disease a marker has been found on the long arm of chromosome 21. Interestingly it is also chromosome 21 which is found in triple form, rather than double, in Down's syndrome. Post-mortem analysis of adults, aged over 25 with Down's syndrome, also reveals neurofibrillary tangles and plaques similar to those seen in Alzheimer's disease. The memories of these older Down's cases have not been systematically investigated. The abnormalities in their brains sometimes appear worse than would be predicted from their behaviour. However, there are also suggestions that once dementia begins in Down's syndrome, its course of deterioration is particularly rapid. To return to Alzheimer's disease, it may be that, in common with many disorders, there is an inherited predisposition which is activated in certain people and not in others. Severe stress is also sometimes suggested as a precipitating factor.

Behaviourally, decline in memory function is one of the earliest symptoms in Alzheimer's disease. Episodic memory processes decline before semantic. As the disease progresses and semantic memory also declines, it leaves intact a variety of other procedural skills. In reading, understanding of text and words declines before pronunciation and word recognition skills. One method of estimating the premorbid intellectual skills of Alzheimer's patients is to test their recognition of a standard set of words of declining frequency. The memory processes involved in knowing what a word means decline *before* the memory stores involved in recognition and identification of words, irrespective of meaning. In practice, this means that Alzheimer's patients will be able to recognize and pronounce irregular words like 'yacht', 'choir', 'debt' and 'gnome' at a stage when understanding of the meaning of these words is impossible.

The chances of developing dementia increase with age. As medicine develops, people live longer, and the proportion of the elderly who live long enough to develop dementia increases. In both Europe and North America the proportion of the population with dementia is rising sharply, creating major social and economic problems. Joining the ranks of this swelling group, AIDS dementia is now the focus of increasing concern. Estimates vary, but as many as 80 per cent of AIDS patients may develop dementia. In some patients, it is one of the earlier features.

Short-Term Memory

The discussion so far has centred upon the processes of memory which in traditional models would be called long-term memory. It is distinguished, in such models, from short-term memory, which is commonly tested by the immediate recall of a series of digits. If someone tells you a telephone number and you keep repeating it to yourself until you can write it down, it is short-term memory which you are using. In short-term memory, unless material is rehearsed, it is forgotten. Baddeley and Hitch (1974) introduced the concept of **working memory**, which has largely replaced that of short-term memory. Working memory is made up of three components: an **articulatory loop**, which permits verbal rehearsal; a **visuo-spatial scratch pad**, which holds non-verbal information; and a **central executor**, which coordinates and controls overall activity. In patients with amnesia and in normal elderly people, short-term memory is intact. In Alzheimer's disease it is reduced.

One of the most obvious behavioural characteristics of somebody with a selective deficit of short-term memory but with normal long-term memory would be difficulty in repetition. Comprehension and production of language would be normal but there would be difficulty with the immediate repetition of a particular sentence or series of words. This pattern of performance is seen in a language disorder called **conduction aphasia**, which used to be interpreted in terms of a disconnection between comprehension systems of language and production systems, associated with lesions around the **arcuate fasciculus**. An alternative view is that it reflects a selective deficit in short-term memory.

In addition to the disorders discussed above, memory is also commonly affected in: Parkinson's disease; epilepsy; Huntington's Chorea; Pick's Disease; multiple infarct dementia; neurosyphilis; Jacob–Creutzfeld's disease; hydrocephalus and encephalitis.

To Conclude

Memory is affected by damage to both diencephalic and hippocampal areas of the midbrain, and the temporal regions of the cortex. It is also affected by alcohol, drugs, poisons, blows to the head, old age and dementia. The patterns of memory performance associated with these disorders suggest a variety of different types of memory and memory processes: short-term and long-term;

episodic and semantic; procedural and declarative; verbal and non-verbal; and category specific. Memory impairments may result from faulty encoding, consolidation or retrieval of any of these memory processes.

Chapter Six :
Visual Recognition and the Brain

The visual information that is received through the eye and interpreted in the brain enables us to move around freely in our day-to-day existence and recognize the objects that are encountered in everyday life. It also enables us to avoid danger, for example, by detecting the movements and speed of cars through which we have to manoeuvre. Presumably, in bygone days, vision was also critical in rapidly identifying potential predators or hostile humans, though its role in the former and the appearance of the latter are altered today. In past times, we used the visual system to help us to identify sources of food.

It is still of use in this way, to enable us to negotiate effectively and select from both supermarket shelves and menus in restaurants. The visual system contributes to our cultural life, enabling us to read works of poetry and literature, appraise art and painting, and enjoy the spectacles of ballet, theatre and opera. Rapid interpretation of visual information is also critical in our day-to-day social interactions both in face recognition, enabling us to identify people we know, and in the interpretation of their facial expressions, which convey information about their moods, attitudes and expectations.

Visual Dependence

Our dependence on vision is conspicuous – observe the rapid deterioration of our movement if the lights go out at a public or social function. In these circumstances, we bump into things, are unable to find what we are looking for and may fail to identify other people. The difference which vision makes to the quality of our social interactions is evident from talking on the telephone, when it is often easier for humans to be deceptive than when they are talking face to face.

The importance attached to vision is evident from the extensive use of electrical and artificial lighting to improve the potential quality of visual information in circumstances where clarity may be reduced. This has enabled the widespread extension of waking and functional hours and enables man to time the activities of the day outside the constraints of daylight. A vast industry has been spawned concerned with producing spectacles, contact lenses and other devices enabling us to maintain and improve the quality of vision as it alters during life. A further range of scientific equipment enables us to extract visual information in greater and greater detail. Electron microscopes have particularly high magnifications by employing electron beams in place of light and using electron lenses.

The capacity of the visual system to keep track and monitor many different sources of visual information at once also contributes to its utility and success. I have a friend who appears able to sew her tapestry, read the newspaper, watch television and conduct a social conversation simultaneously. This kind of behaviour is some distance from the physiological study of vision which focusses on the various cells in the brain which respond to lines of particular angles or orientation.

Processing Information

It was once believed that the visual system processed information in a relatively simple hierarchical fashion. Some of these views arose from the work of Hubel and Wiesel (1962), who investigated the responsiveness of individual cells in the brain to particular stimuli projected on a screen. The term 'visual field' is used to describe the array of visual information which is discernible to our eyes at any moment. Hubel and Wiesel discussed the idea of cells in the brain having particular **receptive fields**, which meant that there were particular areas of the visual field to which they responded. Stimuli within a receptive field could make a particular cell fire and stimuli outside the receptive field might generate no response from the cell, or might inhibit its firing rate. In many cases, Hubel and Wiesel described receptive fields, surrounded by inhibitory areas, which would reduce the activity of the cell. In their hierarchical classification of cells, they described three different types of cell: **simple**, which responded to lines of a particular orientation; **complex**, which responded to lines which were of a particular orientation and in a particular position; and **hyper-complex**, which were somewhat less concerned with position but were concerned about the lengths of lines. We now know that the simple hierarchy which was postulated is not the only mechanism of information transition. Most of the connections between these different types of cells are reciprocal with multiple feedback systems. We also know that not all cells are orientation selective. Only certain zones within the visual regions of the brain have these characteristics.

There is now evidence that different aspects of the visual arrays that we see may be processed through different channels simultaneously. In particular, there is evidence that colour, form, motion, and location are processed in separate parallel channels. Later in the visual system, these sources of information combine to produce the perception of an integrated visual array. Some of the evidence for the independence of these channels comes from studies of patients with brain injury, but before discussing these, it may be informative to say a little more about some of the major projections within the visual system.

Physiology and Anatomy

When light first enters the eye it strikes the retina, which contains different types of ganglion cells. In one specialized pathway (see fig. 6.1.), the anatomists have identified **α cells** which project into the **dorsal lateral geniculate nuclei** to layers which contain large cells, so-called **magnocellular layers**. From here there is a further projection to specific layers of area V1 which is the first area in the cortex to receive visual information and is at the very back of the occipital lobes, right at the back of the head. Information from V1 projects to area V3, which processes information about form, and also to area V5, which is selective to direction and motion. Area V5 is also sometimes referred to as MT. These sources of information can combine in areas sensitive to dynamic form in the parietal lobes. A second major specialized pathway involves **β cells** in the retina. These project to the **parvocellular layers** of the dorsal lateral geniculate nuclei, which have smaller neurons than the magnocellular layers. From the parvocellular layers, there is further projection to different layers of V1. This second specialized pathway then projects to areas V2 and V4, which signal form and colour. There is evidence from the

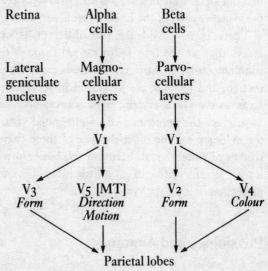

6.1 Parallel visual pathways.

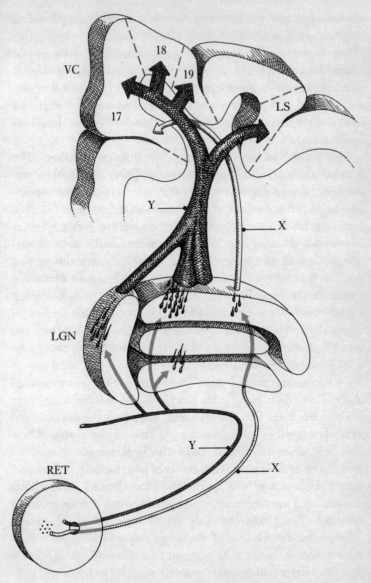

6.2 X and Y cell pathways: RET – retina; LGN – lateral geniculate nuclei; VC – visual cortex.

physiologists that the substrate for the α pathway in the retina involves so-called **Y cells** (see fig. 6.2). These have large receptive fields, respond very quickly, and occur more on the periphery of vision. In contrast, the β cells provide a substrate for the X pathway. Eighty-five per cent of the cells in the foveal region are **X cells**. They have a much slower speed of response and smaller receptive fields. They are, therefore, more tuned to detailed analysis of structure.

The X and Y pathways appear to have different functions. The Y cells, which are distributed on the periphery of vision and are sensitive to rapid movement, may alert you to the sudden appearance of something on the edge of your visual field. You can then turn your head or eye to focus upon the object or person who has appeared and, using the X-cell system, can make detailed discriminations about appearance. It is possible to demonstrate that the Y-cell system is insensitive to colour by bringing a coloured pencil slowly forward from behind your head, whilst looking straight ahead, to a position where it is just possible for you to detect the presence of this object and movement of it before you are able to identify its colour. A change of position or movement of objects attracts our attention. It appears that the visual system divides the detection of these objects from their more detailed analysis. Needless to say, this description of the visual pathways is a simplification. For example, other cells from the dorsal lateral geniculate nucleus may project to layer 1 of the cortex. These may have properties like **W cells** with large receptive fields and slow speed of activation. One per cent of geniculate neurons are intermediate in size between the magnocellular and parvocellular neurons and survive even if the whole visual striate cortex is removed. These cells obviously supply a further visual system. The precise functioning of the latter two systems, and indeed their existence, is not fully substantiated. However, it is possible that the system which survives striate removal provides the abilities which have been reported in some brain-damaged patients who are able to make accurate visual judgements about material which they have no conscious awareness of seeing. This so-called **blindsight** will be discussed later.

In many areas of the visual system cells are organized in **cortical columns**. Some of these columns of cells may be devoted to detecting angles of particular orientation. Inhibition across the cortex in a horizontal direction between the different columns may sharpen their orientation selectivity. There are also groupings of cells sensitive to specific disparities in the visual input coming from each eye and these contribute to our ability to perceive depth.

There are obviously many theories about how we extract from the visual system the information that enables us to recognize a particular pattern. Past theories include **template theory**, which suggested that we establish visual templates in the brain so that we recognize things by matching them exactly to the template. This kind of system would not work very well in the outside world because we frequently encounter objects whose edges are covered or occluded, or which are seen at an unusual angle. It is therefore important that our visual system is able to detect objects even when we only have a partial view of them. Another theory suggested that we use the features of objects and add them together in order to identify the object. Attempts to program computers to recognize objects in this way have shown what a complicated task it is.

Psychophysics

Much of the area which has been called **psychophysics** has been concerned with the idea that we conduct a particular mathematical analysis of the visual input that we receive. This **Fourier analysis** is like sending the visual information we receive through a series of filters or sieves so that we divide it up into different components. The different components are represented as gratings of dark and light lines. Sometimes these are drawn as vertical black and white stripes though, in fact, there is a shading between

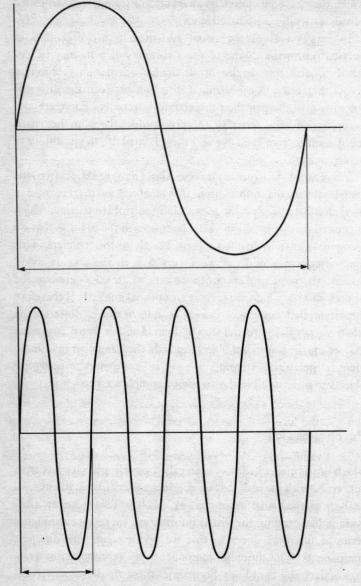

6.3 Sine waves: Wavelengths are illustrated by the arrows.

the edges of the stripes where there is a narrow blend of grey. These gratings are supposed to represent **sine waves**, as illustrated in fig. 6.3. You can think of the top of the sine wave as the black part of the striped pattern and the bottom of the sine wave as the white part of the striped pattern. If you go along the sine wave from the left-hand side to the right, you will go from dark to light with rapid periods of change between the two colours. Sine waves can be of different **frequency**, which means that a different number of them can occur in a fixed period of time (see fig. 6.3). If we have a wave of higher frequency then there are more up-and-down movements within the wave in that period of time. Waves of higher frequency have a shorter **wavelength**. This means that there are more changes in the colour of the grating and so high-frequency sine waves are represented by gratings with very narrow stripes. They are said to be of high-spatial frequency since there is a lot of variation over a short area of space. In contrast, **low-spatial-frequency** information corresponds to sine waves that have very few fluctuations up and down over a period of time. These waves appear wider and are represented by grating patterns in which the stripes are wider. Sine waves can vary not only in how many modulations occur over a period of time but also in the height and depth of the peaks and troughs. The distance from the level on the ground to the peak and trough is referred to as the **amplitude**; the greater the amplitude, the more intense the waves can be considered, with deeper black or white stripes on the gratings.

It is valid to ask why psychophysicists bother to do this sort of manipulation on visual information and why the brain would be interested in utilizing such a mechanism as Fourier analysis. One reason for doing this processing is that different spatial frequencies provide different types of visual information. High-spatial frequencies provide information about the detail of pictures and low-spatial frequencies provide more general information about texture. There is some evidence that cells in the visual system may be more responsive to certain types of spatial frequency and that there may be some selectivity in these responses. These days, some discussions of Fourier analysis take place in the context of discussing a theory which was proposed by Marr (1980) and which retains a great deal of popular appeal. Fourier analysis can be incorporated into the first stage of Marr's theory of visual perception.

Marr's Theory of Visual Perception

This theory is very simple to understand, although the mathematical detail in which Marr writes, about some of the mechanisms involved in the stages, is a little more complicated. In the first stage in his theory, Marr suggests that a **primal sketch** is constructed. This primal sketch identifies intensity changes and edges in a system sensitive to features. Patients who have difficulty with visual recognition are sometimes referred to as **agnosic**. If the nature of the agnosia leads to difficulty in constructing the primal sketch, the patients may exhibit **shape agnosia** where they have difficulty in copying and discriminating between even simple shapes (Humphreys and Riddoch, 1987). Some of these patients may be included within the group of patients described by Lissauer, in 1890, with **apperceptive visual agnosia**. Apperceptive visual agnosics have difficulty with simple copying tasks and matching to sample drawings which they cannot recognize. Some of the shape agnosics described in the literature have suffered from carbon monoxide poisoning, which may have the effect of producing a large number of very small lesions across the visual cortex, resulting in impaired ability to register form sufficiently to construct the primal sketch.

There is a substantial jump in Marr's theory from the primal sketch to his next level of description, the $2\frac{1}{2}$D level, called this because, in many ways, it is nearly a three-dimensional description. It contains the structural description of objects that tells you what they look like. However, the representation is described as being **viewer-centred**. This means that, when the viewer moves, the $2\frac{1}{2}$D representation alters. You can think of this by looking at a chair in the centre of a room. The visual impression which the chair produces alters significantly as you get up and walk to the other side of the room. You retain the impression that it is the same chair and you identify it as such, yet the final visual configuration which the chair is producing is very different from the initial visual configuration. The chair is said to have a different $2\frac{1}{2}$D representation from each of these views. To recognize an object from any angle, including an unfamiliar angle, we must have an abstracted **three-dimensional representation** which is independent of the angle at which it is viewed. These three-dimensional representations are therefore said to be **object-centred** rather than viewer-centred.

Some brain-damaged patients may have difficulty in achieving this three-dimensional level of representation. Patients with parietal lobe lesions, who have been described by Warrington and James (1967) and Warrington and Taylor (1973), may have difficulty with tasks that require recognition from unconventional angles (see fig. 6.4). These patients may also have difficulty in

6.4 Objects viewed from unconventional angles (Warrington, 1982): The parietal lobe is implicated in our ability to identify objects in these views.

recognizing line drawings. This suggests that when the visual information is presented in an unconventional format, or somewhat degraded, it is insufficient for the patient to access the appropriate description of the object. These **transformational agnosias** may result from visual recognition which cannot go beyond the 2½D level, according to Ratcliff and Newcombe (1982). Patients with parietal lobe lesions can recognize most conventionally presented items. Obviously there must be many processing components between the construction of the primal sketch and the activation of the 2½D level.

Gestalt Principles

Possibly involved in the transition from the primal sketch to the 2½D level, gestalt principles describe emergent properties not present in any one item in an array. The illustration of these principles is most simply done by looking at the patterns of dots displayed in fig. 6.5. We see these circles, not as an array of random dots, but as a series of four lines of dots. Our gestalt

· · · · · · ·

· · · · · · ·

· · · · · · ·

6.5 Gestalt perception: These dots are
viewed as lying in four rows.

· · · · · · ·

abilities cause us to group the dots in this way on the basis of their spatial location and relative position. Another integrating principle is the capacity to extract a figure from its ground. In circumstances where this is difficult, as in the ambiguous figure (see fig. 6.6) we can see the difficulty which the system sometimes

6.6 An ambiguous figure: vase or two faces?

6.7 A mooney face (Lansdell, 1968).

encounters. The capacity to make rapid gestalt integration and produce closure over a visual array does not seem to correlate in any simple way with intelligence. However, several neuropsychological tests attempt to measure these capacities since they are thought to be important in perceptual processes. An example of a test item of this sort is the face depicted in fig. 6.7. With this task, the subject is required to indicate whether the picture is of an elderly person, an adult or a child and also to indicate the sex of the person. The subject is told that what they are looking at is a face and they must make specific judgements about it. These judgements cannot be made, unless the different black and white elements which depict the face are integrated together. In other tests, the subject must actually identify the object that is depicted. These tests can be even harder, as illustrated in the example in fig. 6.8.

Gestalt principles are not simply concerned with form. They

6.8 Gestalt perception: Integration of the fragmentary elements is necessary in order to see this as a house.

also concern movement. If you switch on and off two lights in nearby locations, such that each light alternates between being on and then off, the observer perceives a single light moving back and forth. This is referred to as the **illusion of movement**. Gestalt theory includes the **concept of Pragnanz**, which says that the visual system converges on the most logical, regular and symmetrical perception that is consistent with the sensory information which it receives. Gestalt laws can be based on similarity, as illustrated in fig. 6.9. The ambiguity of visual perception and the

6.9 The Gestalt law of similarity: Although the dots are of similar size and number, we see two separate groups on the basis of their similarity.

use of gestalt principles is incorporated often into art. Many artistic representations are sufficiently similar to things which we have previously perceived that we are able to extract some kind of content or meaning from them. However, they may be sufficiently different to make them interesting, novel and stimulating.

The output of the 3D level of representation is integrated with so-called **object recognition units** which, in current models, contain the stores of previously observed objects and enable us to recognize both new examples of familiar objects and also a specific chair or painting that we have seen before. These recognition units seem to contain information about the structural description and the appearance of the object. In order for us to actually recognize what it is, we must integrate this with some **semantic knowledge** about what objects are actually like. Brain-damaged patients who have difficulty in making this transition might be perfectly able to make a decision about whether something is an object but are unable to generate appropriate associations to it. Elements of their world may seem as though there are many unfamiliar, though clear and visible, objects placed around them. In this sense, they see the objects but they do not recognize them. This type of disorder is referred to as **associative agnosia**. Some associative agnosias can arise from damage to the store of knowledge that we have about the world itself. This can be seen in the latter stages of profound memory impairment and dementia, when the semantic store of information gradually deteriorates. These patients are sometimes referred to as **semantic agnosics**.

Warrington (1982) has pointed out that disturbances of the semantic system could lead directly to agnosic difficulties. She studied cases of visual agnosia in the presence of memory impairment and word-finding difficulties but with only mild intellectual deficit. The patients were shown a series of pictures of animals and rather than being asked to identify the animal, they were asked questions like 'Which is the largest?' Alternatively, the animal was put in an array with other items and they were asked

'Which is the animal?' Warrington's patients had difficulty even with these verbal questions, requiring the use of semantic knowledge. If the knowledge of an object has deteriorated and if there is only one such store in the brain, then there will be difficulties in recognition, regardless of the modality of the sensory input. Where agnosic deficits result from inability to access semantic information itself, then the recognition difficulties should also appear when identifying items by touch or smell. The tactile or olfactory information still needs to be integrated with knowledge of the world, if it is to be recognized. These types of agnosic difficulties have also been described in patients who have had **viral herpes encephalitis**. The virus produces diffuse damage through the temporal lobes in both hemispheres which may cause the deterioration of semantic knowledge. We know that the temporal lobes and underlying hippocampi normally have an integral function in memory processing. Some scientists disagree with the idea that there is a single semantic system and argue that there are multiple semantic systems, with a different semantic system for each type of sensory input. However, the evidence for this is far from conclusive.

If a neurological patient is presented with something to name and is unable to name it, it does not necessarily mean that they have agnosia. There could be something wrong with their eyes which affects the sensory information itself. More commonly, if there is no sensory defect, there could be a language disorder which makes it difficult for the patient to access the name of the object, even if the object itself has been correctly identified and recognized. In this case, the difficulty is not perceptual. The patient will be able to indicate the use of the object and also sometimes give a roundabout description called a **circumlocution**, which lets the tester know that they have indeed recognized the object. These sorts of disorders are referred to as **anomias** rather than agnosias and were mentioned in Chapter Four.

When agnosic patients are unable to recognize objects, they can nevertheless usually indicate where the object is and they can tell you if the object moves. Thus, visual information about location and movement are intact. Frequently they can also indicate the colour of the object. This supports the view that the channels involved with identifying objects differ from those which are used in the detection of movement, location or colour. Occasionally, the reverse pattern is seen. There are descriptions of unusual patients, who are able to recognize objects, therefore showing intact form perception, but who have difficulty with the detection of movement. One such case is described by Zihl, von Cramon and Mai (1983). The patient was able to see objects quite clearly, but if the object moved she saw what appeared as a series of still frames in a slow-moving film, so that people or objects appeared to jump from one location to another. This created particular difficulties if she was attempting to pour liquid into a cup, since she would see several frames but then might miss the frame which included the cup almost overflowing with liquid, so that she was unable to stop pouring at the appropriate time. It also made it difficult for her to cross the road because she could not judge the movements of cars.

If our visual system is working efficiently, we must not only be able to direct attention to moving parts of the visual field, but we should also be able to filter out movement. We need to be able to see both movement against a stationary background and also an item moving in one direction against a background moving in a different direction. When driving a car along a motorway, it is essential to differentiate easily the movement of our own car and the flow of traffic in one direction from the movement of the other cars coming in the opposite direction. Both of these should be distinguishable from the background, which appears to be moving across the retina, but which is in reality static. The patient described by Zihl *et al* has been further investigated by McCloud *et al* (1989), who show that she is unable to filter out movement. In this patient there are bilateral lesions to areas V_5, also called MT, so MT is probably the site of the movement filter used in normal visual processing.

Colour Perception

The visual system involved in the perception of colour and lumin-
ance can also be selectively affected by brain damage. This
breakdown occurs at a fairly early stage of the colour recognition
process. The patients may experience achromatopsia, in which
they wake up and suddenly perceive the world in black and
white. Otherwise the visual system appears to work normally and
so this does not tend to be a long-term handicapping condition.
With damage in areas further into the visual cortex, the patients
may experience colour agnosia in which they are unable to recognize colours (Davidoff, 1991). This is most easily demonstrated by getting the patient to colour in a black-and-white
line drawing containing objects which have characteristic colours, for example a bowl of fruit containing apples, grapes,
strawberries and plums. The patient will select the wrong
colour of pencils and will produce a coloured drawing in which
the fruit do not match their natural colour. Colour recognition
disorders could also result from damage to the semantic system,
if the patient has, for example, lost the knowledge that bananas
are yellow.

The survival value of the brain's ability to identify colour is
less evident in today's society, but the subtle influence of colour
on our perception appears to have effects of which we are not
aware. For example, you are least likely to be hit by another car
on the road if you drive a red car and most likely if you drive a
green car. Green, of course, is a more common background colour,
being associated with countryside and nature, whereas red is the
colour of blood. Red may be something which produces increased
alertness. In fact, the brain responds to red light in a different
way to how it responds to blue light. Amongst the small percentage of people who have **photosensitive epilepsies**, which are
triggered by particular light patterns and visual configurations,
some are influenced by the colour of the light which is producing

stimulation. Blue patterns are less likely to induce these people to have an epileptic seizure than red patterns. The visual patterns which induce these seizures usually contain stripes or repeated patterns. Some people's first epileptic seizure is triggered in a situation where they are exposed to stripes or flicker. This can be the stroboscopic lights of a discotheque, the flicker of a television screen, the shifting striped pattern of a moving escalator, or the striped pattern of moving text as we read down the page of a book. The patterns which are most likely to induce this epileptic response can also create mild headache and migraine effects in other sensitive individuals. The patterns have similar structure to the patterns generated in a migraine, if there is a visual perceptual illusion created during the attack. Similar patterns are described by some people who have taken LSD and by American Indians taking the drug peyote. In some ways the structure of these patterns appears to tie intimately to the physiology of the brain.

Face Recognition

The brain's response to other complex visual patterns has been investigated in studies of **face recognition**, which is an important social skill bestowing a certain advantage upon those who find the task easy. There could be an evolutionary benefit in having an advanced skill in this direction, both to distinguish people in one's own community and to distinguish them readily from others. There continues to be an argument about whether there are specialized face-recognition mechanisms in the brain, or whether other visually complex objects with mutual similarity in appearance are recognized using the same mechanisms. In these studies, the attempts to construct sets of visually similar stimuli for comparison with faces are not very successful. Some people compare face recognition with recognition of the fronts of cars or famous buildings. However, there are clearly individual differences and cultural variations in the capacity to perform either of these latter tasks. It is known, from single-cell recording in monkeys, that there are cells in the infero-temporal cortex which respond specifically to faces and hands. In humans, bilateral damage in this area can lead to **prosopagnosia**, in which there is difficulty in recognizing faces.

Several types of difficulty in face recognition are documented in the neurological literature. Difficulty with early perceptual processes in face recognition was described by Bodamer (1947). His patient thought that a picture of a dog was an unusually hairy human being. Bodamer also mentioned **metamorphopsia**, in which the face looks distorted but can be recognized. Both of these disorders may result from difficulty in the **structural encoding** of faces, required before accessing the **face recognition units** which represent stores of familiar faces. Nowadays the patient described by Bodamer would tend not to be called a prosopagnosic. In current use of the term prosopagnosia, the patients are able to recognize that a face is a face but they cannot identify the face. It is the association of the precept with its meaning which is problematic.

Bruyer *et al* (1983) have described a fifty-year-old farmer who had bilateral occipital lobe lesions. This man appeared to have defective operation of face-recognition units. He was able to pick out human faces from animals, cars and houses, and could copy line drawings of faces. He could also match unfamiliar faces and discriminate between faces of familiar people. So the farmer was able to establish an adequate visual percept, yet he was unable to recognize famous faces, friends, family, hospital staff, and even himself. Although these recognition difficulties occurred with faces, he was able to recognize people from names and from voices. There was thus an impairment in accessing recognition from the information about visual configuration but there was no disorder in the memory for people themselves. In current models of face recognition, the stores of memory for people are referred to as **person-identity nodes**. These are supposed to contain information that you have about people that you know.

Amnesic patients may have difficulty in identifying people from names, as well as faces. Here the person-identity nodes have been eroded along with the general deterioration of memory. There is also a strange disorder which is called the **Capgrass syndrome**. Here the patients will claim that their family has been replaced by another family who look similar to their own. The timing of the replacement is coincident with the brain damage which the person has sustained. Thus, in some sense, people must look familiar to these patients and yet, in some other critical sense, they appear to have lost some element of personal recognition. Inevitably, all of these difficulties with face recognition are problematic for the patient.

In order to get around the difficulties with face recognition, patients attempt to use various strategies to recognize people. For example, they may notice the clothes they wear, their hairstyle, their walk or their voice. Face-recognition difficulties can be very conspicuous, both to relatives and friends and to the clinician. At the beginning of a clinical session, a doctor or psychologist may spend time establishing rapport with the patient. When they next encounter the patient, the patient may act as if they have never met before, yet it will become apparent that they remember the content of the session that has taken place. It is the recognition of the individual from their face which is defective.

Such specific difficulties with face recognition can also be found in developmental forms, though they are much less documented and little discussed. In developmental form the child is unable, or has difficulty with, recognizing familiar faces and this difficulty extends through life (Temple, 1992). This produces many social problems and difficulties in negotiating the world which are not necessarily immediately apparent. Such disorders tend not to be picked up in any conventional way by screening at school. Since there is little information about them, there might also be difficulty in having them accurately recognized, even by professionals. Yet these children have significance for understanding brain mechanisms for face recognition, since they indicate that there is a modular organization in the development of perceptual and recognition systems.

Studies suggest that some neurological patients with impairments of face recognition have a greater knowledge about faces than they realize. For example, De Haan, Young and Newcombe (1987a, b) studied a face-recognition disorder in a subject who had had a head injury following a motorcycle accident, at the age of nineteen. Their subject, *P.H.*, was able to match different views of unfamiliar faces and could recognize people from their names, suggesting that both the initial structural encoding of faces and the person–identity nodes for people are intact. Nevertheless, he was unable to recognize faces. De Haan set out three further studies, to look at whether there might be any unconscious face-recognition ability.

He presented pairs of faces and asked *P.H.* whether they were the same or a different person. *P.H.* was faster with familiar faces than with unfamiliar faces. He also gave *P.H.* the 'bubble' task. In this, the patient must make a judgement about whether or not a particular name is a politician or a TV personality. The names are presented in cartoon-style bubbles coming out of the mouths of pictures of these people (see fig. 6.10). In some cases, the face and the name are the same person, in others the face and the name are of related people in the field, and in the final case the face and name are unrelated. The subject is told to ignore the faces and just judge the names. *P.H.*'s reaction times to answer were fastest if both the name and the face came from the same person. They were at an intermediate level if the face and the name were related and they were slowest if the face and the name were unrelated. Yet, if *P.H.* were given the faces and asked simply to sort them into two different categories of politicians and TV personalities, his performance was entirely at chance. In face-memory tasks, *P.H.* also found it easier to learn the name of a famous face if it were a true association rather than a false one. The familiarity of faces influences his performance on the 'bubble' task and the memory task but he is unable to use this informa-

6.10 The bubble task: Stimuli for which the name is congruent with the picture are normally faster to judge.

tion in any overt fashion. If it were possible in some way to harness these unconscious face-recognition abilities, it might be possible to develop a remedial system to bypass the major deficit.

Implicit recognition had previously been documented in patients who had bilateral occipital damage and considered themselves blind (Weiskrantz, 1986). They were requested to make simple discriminations of circles and crosses and were also asked to point to the location of stimuli. These tasks were performed at a level above chance despite the patients' beliefs that they were simply guessing wildly, therefore, the condition is referred to as **blindsight**. However, the level of perceptual discrimination which is required to identify a face is more sophisticated than that which is required to discriminate a circle from a cross. De Haan's studies suggest that the level of unconscious access to visual information can be more sophisticated than that seen in blind-sight.

Chapter Seven
Reading and Writing and the Brain

Reading, writing and arithmetic all use formal codes which are learnt by cultural instruction. These systems enable us to record and decode information so that we are not completely dependent on our memories to recall things. They also enabled the transition of information and ideas from one generation to another, in days before the more sophisticated electronic gadgetry of the late twentieth century. We can read the ideas and stories of authors who have been dead for several hundred years; we can get an impression from their work, not only of the society in which they lived, but also of their own beliefs and aspirations. Reading these works shows us how many of the issues that concern us in our own day to day life also concerned previous generations. Shakespearian sonnets and plays encompass many of the substantive issues that we discuss today. Moreover, they communicate a humour and a perception which, without the written word, we would not otherwise find accessible. However, when we look at a Shakespearian play, we find that certain elements of what is written may be difficult to understand since they reflect aspects of language that have changed over the centuries.

Formal reading and writing codes also enable us to transmit factual and scientific information from generation to generation. They permit us to have ready access to research, investigations and news from different parts of the world in an accessible code. Thus, each new generation is not required to reinvent discoveries which cannot be passed on face-to-face within the culture.

Until comparatively recently, it was not the norm for every

member of the society to learn these formal codes of representation. These skills were acquired frequently by a select group of the society who thereby attained greater power. In the twentieth century, in Western cultures, every child is required to learn to read, spell and do basic calculations. Many children have difficulty in acquiring these skills and the variations in their acquisition partly contribute to the interest in the brain mechanisms which underlie these formal codes.

Whilst English is an international language with a particular written system associated with it, the alphabetic orthography of English is not the only possible structure for a writing system. We believe that written codes were introduced into man's repertoire of skills and abilities after the human brain had fully evolved. Thus, any brain mechanisms involved in reading and writing must have evolved for some other purpose. The history of writing systems seems to be based on early drawings called **pictograms**, each of which is a direct image of the object it represents. The relation between the meaning of the symbol and its form is not arbitrary. This type of representational system is still used in some areas today and is also employed in some international symbols, thus some international road signs are clearly pictograms (see fig. 7.1). Since the pictogram symbol relates to the shape of the object, the particular pronunciation of the word in the language is irrelevant.

7.1 The representational system of pictograms still used in some international road signs.

Over time, the meaning of the pictogram was extended to represent not only the object but attributes of concepts associated with it. Thus, a pictogram of the sun could come to represent concepts of warmth and heat. In this transition, pictograms came to represent ideas and were called **ideograms**, which later became stylized abstractions. The simplifying conventions distorted the representations so that it was no longer possible to interpret the symbols without actually having explicit instructions about the system. Now the relationship between the actual shape of the symbol and its meaning has become arbitrary and we have linguistic symbols.

The oldest writing system known is that of the Sumerians, who lived in southern Mesopotamia about 5,000 years ago. They were traders and, as their business became more successful and extensive, a need arose for permanent records of their transactions. They established an elaborate pictograph system and an elaborate system of tallies, to represent numerical values. Over the centuries the characters came to be produced by a wedge-shaped implement in clay and these symbols are referred to as **cuneiforms**, which means wedge-shaped (see fig. 7.2). The cuneiform script was borrowed by the Assyrians and, later, by the Persians. However, when the Assyrians and Persians adopted the symbols, they used them to represent the sounds of syllables.

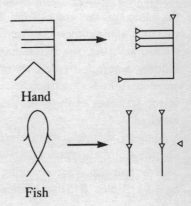

Hand

Fish

7.2 Cuneiforms.

At the same time as the Sumerians were using a pictograph system, a similar system was developed by the Egyptians, which later became called **hieroglyphics**, *hiero* meaning sacred and *glyphikos* meaning carving (see fig. 7.3). Although originally they were pictographs, they came to represent sounds. Syllabic representations were used when the symbols were borrowed by other people.

7.3 Hieroglyphics.

In the tenth century BC, the Greeks borrowed this symbolic system, but syllables were rather inefficient to represent their language. In the Semitic languages, from which the symbols came, there are many monosyllabic words and polysyllabic words with simple and regular syllables. However, Greek had a complex syllabic structure and required a very large number of symbols, if a different symbol was to represent each syllable. The Greeks took the symbols of the Phoenician system but used them to represent individual sounds, and also introduced symbols to represent vowels as well as consonants.

Our own writing system is derived from the Greek system and the name alphabet comes from the first two Greek letters of the alphabet, *alpha* and *beta*. In fact, our alphabet is derived from the Roman alphabet, which was introduced to England in the sixth century, whereas the derivatives of the Greek Cyrillic alphabet are modern Russian scripts. Standardization of spelling took place in the sixteenth century and was relatively stable by seventeen hundred.

Modern writing systems include both the Roman and the Cyrillic alphabetic system, in which symbols represent individual sounds, and also syllabic writing systems, in which symbols represent syllables. Syllabic writing systems include certain Indian languages such as Devanagari and also certain portions of Japanese script. Japanese script has an interesting structure because it is made up of two different sections. The syllabic section is referred to as **kana** and is used to represent foreign words in the language and also to represent the grammatical markings in the language, such as word endings and tenses. There are two different types: **hiragana** which is a cursive kana; and **katakana**, which is a square kana (see fig. 7.4). It is the hiragana that marks the gram-

	ス	セ	ソ	サ	タ	ナ
Katakana	su	se	so	sa	ta	na

	た	つ	て	ち		
Hiragana	ta	tu	te	ti		

7.4 Examples of Japanese script: katakana and hiragana.

matical features and the katakana that is used for the imported words and non-Japanese proper names. It is also used to give emphasis, so in some ways it is like the italics of English. Another portion of Japanese script is logographic. This section is called **kanji**. Kanji symbols are ideographic and are borrowed from Chinese; modern Chinese is composed almost exclusively of these symbols. Kanji characters represent a particular concept. The basic symbol or radical for *tree* would also be found in the kanji representations of words such as *desk*, *timber*, *twig*, *board* and *pine*. Similarly, the basic kanji radical for *speech* and *language* would also be found in the representations for *story*, *word*, *correction*, *translation* and *poetry* (see fig. 7.5). These more complex kanjis are based on combinations of radicals. Whenever brain mechanisms are involved in processing reading and spelling, they must permit the use of these different types of writing systems by different cultures.

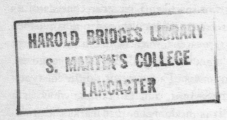

言　Language

話　Story

詩　Poetry

語　Word

証　Evidence

7.5 Examples of Japanese script: kanji.

Many contemporary cognitive models of how the brain carries out the operations of reading and spelling are derived from the work of Morton (1979), which began with studies of context effects. Morton would present sentences to subjects and ask them to complete the sentences. He found that some endings were common responses for people to make and some were less common. So, for example, if presented with the sentence 'They went to see the new –', then *film* is the common response and *picture* the infrequent response. With a different sentence, 'They looked intently at the –', then *picture* is the common response and *film* the infrequent response. Morton then looked to see how long it would take to recognize a word. He found that the word could be recognized more rapidly if it was preceded by one of the context sentences; moreover, if the word was a common response to the incomplete sentence, then recognition was even more rapid. From these experiments he concluded that visual recognition of words relates to the frequency of probability that the word is going to occur.

The Logogen System

Morton introduced a biological analogy in his models of recognition of written words. He suggested that when we look at a word we add up evidence from it, to see if it matches our stored representation of what the word is like. This store consists of a set of responses which he refers to as **logogens**. He derived the word from the Greek *logos*, meaning word, and *genus*, meaning birth. Just as nerve cells collate different inhibitory and excitatory inputs so that, if stimulation reaches a sufficient threshold level, the nerve cell will fire, so the logogen collates information and, if it reaches a threshold of activation, then the word associated with the logogen will be triggered as a response. Logogens are seen as having all or none response systems, just as neurons were. More common words, or words which are anticipated, will have lower thresholds of activation and will therefore be triggered more easily. Thus, in his discussions of the variations in the response levels of his logogens, Morton also borrows ideas from variations in ease of neuronal activation. The simplest way to account for frequency effects, in which it is easier to recognize common words, is to say that the threshold of a logogen is permanently reduced by a small amount every time the logogen is active. Exposure to common words gradually reduces their threshold of activation. Each logogen is only effective for one word. In fact, more precisely, logogens represent **morphemes** rather than words, a morpheme being a minimal unit of meaning in a language. Thus, in reading the word *sing*, *singing* and *singer*, the same logogen for *sing* is activated and the affixes to the words, the grammatical endings, are processed separately. Work from experimental psychology indicates that the affixes are **stripped** from the words prior to identification (Taft, 1981). Their pronunciations are then re-attached after recognition. This is a process of which we are unaware.

Picture-recognition systems are quite separate from the visual logogen system that Morton describes. However, when very young children first start to learn to read they may use the picture-recognition system in the early stages, until more sophisticated systems are developed.

The brain's expectations influence the actions of the logogen system. There are many errors in public signs, which both the person who made the sign and passers-by often fail to notice. Their prior expectations of what the sequence of words will say affects their ability to detect errors. Examples of this are given in fig. 7.6.

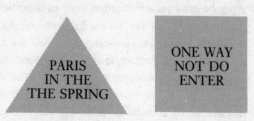

7.6 Signs with missed errors.

The reading system can also be confused by conflicting information. Experiments using Stroop stimuli were mentioned in Chapter Two in relation to the frontal lobes. Colour names are written in ink, of a different colour to the name, for example, the word *green* is written in blue ink and the word *red* is written in yellow ink. The subject is asked to name the colours as quickly as possible. The time taken is compared with the time to name colour stimuli which are sequences of crosses rather than the names of colours. The colour naming is found to be slowed down by the competing colour name.

Morton's logogen system is an early stage in current reading models. Following activation of the appropriate logogen, the meaning of the word is triggered which, in turn, triggers the word's pronunciation. This reading system is called a **lexical reading route** or a **semantic reading route**, since recognition of the word proceeds via its meaning or semantics. We must also have a second kind of reading system, since we are able to read out loud nonsense words or unfamiliar words and work out what they pronounce. So, for example, if asked the written question 'Does a yott have a sail?' most people would be able to answer. We could also read the sentence 'The phoks ran away' and could describe the animal. These abilities show that in addition to the logogen system which recognizes the overall appearance of a word, we must also have a system which is based upon the letter to sound rules, which underpin our alphabetic writing system. This system is called a **phonological reading route**. Thus, contemporary models of reading include at least two routes by which a word may be read aloud: a semantic reading route and a phonological reading route (see fig. 7.7).

In the semantic reading route, following visual analysis, the word triggers a response in the **visual-input logogen system**. This activates a meaning associated with the word in the **semantic**

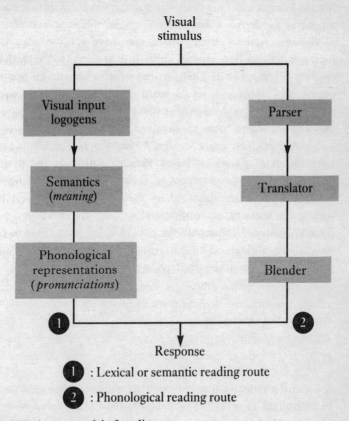

7.7 A dual-route model of reading.

system and the pronunciation of the word activates from a store of **phonological representations**. These responses are then held in a buffer and can either be spoken aloud or not. In the phonological reading route, following visual analysis, the written-letter string is dissected by a **parser** into segments. Each of these graphemic segments of letters is translated to a phonemic segment of sounds, then the sounds are blended together to produce an overall pronunciation. Models which incorporate these two routes are referred to as dual-route models of reading. This type of abstract model might appear to bear little relationship to the human brain itself. However, one objective in constructing such a model is to derive a better idea of the different components of the underlying system, which may have specific anatomical locations. Blood flow studies support a multiple route model to reading (Petersen *et al*, 1988) within which extra-striate occipital cortex may represent visual word forms and input logogens; temporo-parietal regions may be involved in phonological processing; and left frontal areas are involved in semantic associations.

There has been other evidence that the two reading routes have different anatomical bases. Patients with acquired dyslexia have had normal development of their reading and spelling systems, but these are damaged as the result of brain injury or disease. In some cases, reading and spelling are eliminated completely, but more commonly the patient is left with some reading or spelling abilities. The pattern of the abilities that are left provides clues about the underlying structure of the system.

Acquired Dyslexias

Deep Dyslexia

A lot of the recent interest in patients with acquired dyslexia can be attributed to a revival which followed the study of Marshall and Newcombe (1966) of a case of deep dyslexia. They described a patient, *G.R.*, who had sustained a missile injury during the Second World War. The most interesting feature of *G.R.*'s performance was the incidence of particular types of error. In these, *G.R.* would read a word as one that was similar in meaning, though not in appearance or sound. So, for example, *G.R.* might read the word *gnome* as 'pixie'. Alternatively he might read the word *black* as 'white'. These errors are called **semantic paralexias** because there is a relationship in meaning between the stimulus and the response (see fig. 7.8). Since *G.R.* was able to

demon → 'Satan'	*spectacles* → 'binoculars'
guilty → 'judge'	*tartan* → 'kilt'
merry → 'happy'	*paddock* → 'kennel'
fortune → 'riches'	*navy* → 'sailor'
thirsty → 'drink'	*beauty* → 'love'
pair → 'two'	*genealogist* → 'babies'

7.8 Semantic errors made by deep dyslexics when reading single words aloud.

access an element of underlying meaning, Marshall and New-combe thought of the deep structure of meaning which Chomsky has suggested underlies spoken language. They therefore called the reading syndrome shown by *G.R.* **deep dyslexia**.

Although initial scepticism greeted the description of the patient by Marshall and Newcombe, there have been many subsequent descriptions of similar patients and there is now no doubt that these error patterns are not uncommon. Since the patients are able to access a word similar in meaning to the target, then an element of the original word's meaning must have been processed correctly. Yet they seem to have no access to the sound-based elements of the word. It is as if they are reading with a semantic reading system in the absence of a phonological reading system.

Fifty per cent of *G.R.*'s reading errors to single words were semantic paralexias. Young children and adults reading at speed also make occasional semantic paralexias when reading connected text, but for *G.R.* the semantic errors arose reading isolated words, presented with no other associated information. The deep dyslexic is not simply guessing from the previous context about the word's identity.

Other errors in deep dyslexia are consistent with the idea of semantic route reading. They find it easier to read words that are common and words that are easily imaged, that is, words for which it is easy to imagine a picture, or a sound, or a smell in your mind. So, for example, words like *fire* and words like *chair* are highly **imageable**. These words have a lot of concrete meaning and strong semantic representation. A semantic reading route may find them easy to trigger. More abstract words with less imageable meanings are harder for deep dyslexics to read. For these words the semantic reading route may have a less elaborated representation. Deep dyslexics also find it easier to read words that are of high frequency, that is, words that are very common. This is consistent with the idea that the logogen system finds it easier to trigger words that are very frequent. Deep dyslexics make two further types of error. When reading words that have grammatical endings, they show a tendency to drop these endings off or to substitute them for another ending. Thus, they might read the word *governor* as 'governs'. In the initial descriptions in the literature, these errors were called **derivational paralexias**. Then linguists pointed out that the label was being used to include **inflectional errors**, for example, *sing* as 'singing'. So, in the more recent literature, the term **morphological paralexia** is employed (see fig. 7.9). These variations in terminology are common in this area and can make the academic literature fairly inaccessible. Deep dyslexics also tend to substitute the short grammatical words in the language for each other. So they might read *in* as 'to' or *he* as 'us'. These errors are called **function**

baker → 'bakery'	*truth* → 'true'
beauty → 'beautiful'	*shove* → 'shovel'
marriage → 'married'	*speak* → 'speech'
slavery → 'slaves'	*batting* → 'bat'
acknowledge → 'knowledge'	*apart* → 'part'
courage → 'courageous'	*burn* → 'burnt'

7.9 Morphological paralexias made by deep dyslexics when reading single words aloud.

word substitutions. One theory for the basis of both morphological errors and function word substitutions is that the sound-based rules of reading, incorporated in the phonological reading route, are particularly important in distinguishing between short letter strings, which have little intrinsic meaning, but provide grammatical markings (Patterson, 1982). An alternative view is that a separate and distinct reading system, responsible for processing grammatical elements, is also disrupted in deep dyslexia.

We know that deep dyslexics are unable to use any of the phonological reading system as they are unable to read aloud unfamiliar words or non-words with simple pronunciations, for example, *gip* or *sut*. These letter strings do not mean anything, but for most people it would be relatively easy to work out a logical pronunciation for them. The deep dyslexic cannot work out a word's pronunciation unless it has meaning.

A further reason for the interest in deep dyslexics was because many of the features of their reading performance are very similar to the reading performance described for the right hemisphere of the split-brain patients. In Chapter Three we discussed the corpus callosum and the patients who have been studied following section of this fibre tract as a treatment for chronic epilepsy. Zaidel (1978) has studied the reading performance of both the left and the right hemispheres in these patients. Although the left is the traditional language hemisphere, he found that some right hemispheres had reading ability, but the reading skills are of a specific nature. The right hemisphere does not have phonological reading skills, so it does not have a phonological reading route and cannot pronounce unfamiliar words or non-words. Moreover, amongst the overt errors that they make in reading words, semantic paralexias are common. Their limited reading ability concentrates on words that are highly imageable and also of high frequency.

This similarity in the reading performance of the disconnected right hemispheres of the split-brain patients, and of the deep dyslexic patients who had sustained brain injuries, led Coltheart (1980) to suggest that deep dyslexics are reading with their right hemispheres. Supporters of this view have pointed to the very large area of brain damage in the left hemisphere of the patients who have brain injuries which result in deep dyslexia. They suggest that in some cases there could be very little left hemisphere intact to support reading performance and that take-over by the right hemisphere is probable. This view is supported by occasional studies of hemispherectomy patients. In left hemispherectomy, at least two-thirds of the left hemisphere is surgically removed as a treatment for a particular form of intractable epilepsy. The remaining right hemisphere is sometimes able to read and the pattern of reading is remarkably similar to that of patients with deep dyslexia (Patterson, Vargha-Khadem and Polkey, 1989). However, other researchers argue that in deep dyslexia we are seeing the residual functioning of a bit of the left hemisphere, which is sufficient to generate part of the reading system. This issue is not fully resolved but with the increasing use of more sophisticated brain scanners addressing active metabolism it may be possible to answer this question with greater confidence.

Surface Dyslexia

Deep dyslexia is not the only type of acquired dyslexia which has been of interest to researchers. Marshall and Newcombe (1973) published another paper, in which they compared the performance of their deep dyslexic, *G.R.*, with a second patient, *J.C.*, who had a very different type of reading performance. *J.C.* was also a patient who had previously been able to read very well, but who had suffered from a missile injury in the war. *G.R.* and *J.C.* were of roughly comparable ages, with a similar aetiology to their injuries, although different areas of the brain had been affected. *J.C.* also had reading difficulty, but whereas *G.R.* had made semantic paralexias, these were not made by *J.C.* Instead, *J.C.* had particular difficulty in reading words with irregular spelling-to-sound patterns. These included words like *yacht*, which, if pronounced aloud by a system of letter-sound rules, would sound a bit like 'yatched'. The correct reading of yacht would fit more logically with the spelling *yot*. Similarly, the word *sweat* would have as its most logical reading 'sweet'. These words, like yacht and sweat, are referred to as **irregular** words; when patients like *J.C.* read them it is as if a systematic rule system has been applied and they say 'yatched' or 'sweet'. These errors are called **regularization errors**. In experiments the patients are tested on lists of words which are matched for word frequency, length, part of speech and other relevant linguistic dimensions, so that the word lists differ only in whether they are regular or irregular. The patients show a **regularity effect**, such that the regular list is read better than the irregular list. The deep dyslexic seems to be able to access meaning but not pronunciation, whereas patients like *J.C.* show the opposite pattern, able to access pronunciation but not necessarily meaning. They can read non-words and unfamiliar regular words well. They appear to be using a phonological reading route with an ineffective semantic reading route. Marshall and Newcombe called this second pattern **surface dyslexia**.

For anybody exploring the literature on the acquired dyslexias the terminology for these disorders is very confusing. Marshall and Newcombe specifically focussed on the features which their dyslexic patients retained, naming deep dyslexia as such, since the patients appear to have access to the deep meanings and associations of the words and surface dyslexia as such, because the patient had access to the surface pronunciation. Other researchers have named these disorders in relation to the aspect of the reading system which is lost. Each of these dyslexic disorders, therefore, has several different names. Deep dyslexia is also called **phonemic dyslexia** and surface dyslexia is called **semantic dyslexia**, but deep dyslexia and surface dyslexia are the most common names.

Surface dyslexia has another integral feature. The story told is that Coltheart was travelling on a train through Italy, having discussions with another neuropsychologist about surface dyslexia. They realized that if a surface dyslexic is reliant upon sounding out a word in order to identify it, then words which sound the same but have different spellings will create particular problems. The homophonic words *sale* and *sail* sound the same when read aloud. If the only means to identify these words is from their sound then it will be difficult to distinguish between them.

Coltheart returned to England and tested his patients on sets of homophones. He was interested in the meanings which the patients attributed to each word. He would ask them what the written word *sale* meant and what the written word *sail* meant. When he did this, his surface dyslexics showed **homophone confusion**. When they were asked what *sale* meant, they might say that 'it's somewhere where goods are sold at a reduced price and bargains are found', but they might also say that 'it's something that helps a boat to go along water in the wind'. Their selection between these responses appears random. The only way a surface dyslexic can work out a word's meaning is by first working out its sound. Deep dyslexics who are not concerned about the sound of a word but are concerned about its overall structure do not show any homophone confusion.

The initial interpretation of deep dyslexia and surface dyslexia was that each represented impairment of one of the two reading routes which we have discussed above. Since each reading route could be selectively damaged the anatomical basis must be distinct. In deep dyslexia, the patients have lost the ability to use the phonological reading route, but their lexical and semantic reading route is also generating semantic errors. Some researchers wondered whether there was intrinsic instability in the semantic reading system, which would always cause the generation of semantic errors, in the absence of sound-based cues (Newcombe and Marshall, 1980). Other researchers thought that perhaps in deep dyslexia the semantic reading route itself had also been damaged, so that the patients were reading with only part of the semantic reading route and that this was creating the semantic errors. In the latter case it would predict that purer patients could exist with damaged phonological reading routes but relatively intact semantic reading routes. The patients would be unable to read aloud short pronounceable nonsense words since they would not have phonological reading skills, but they would have good word recognition skills without contamination from semantic errors. This further variety of acquired dyslexia was explicitly predicted from the thinking about deep dyslexia and surface dyslexia. Derouesne and Beauvois (1979) found it in some French patients. The disorder has subsequently been labelled as **phonological dyslexia**.

Phonological Dyslexia

In many ways phonological dyslexia resembles deep dyslexia. The patients have difficulty in reading aloud non-words. They also tend to make morphological paralexias in which the base of the word is read correctly, but an affix is dropped, added or substituted. However, they do not make the semantic errors which are characteristic of deep dyslexia and their overall reading levels are higher than those in deep dyslexia. Phonological dyslexia is therefore interpreted as competent reading by the semantic reading route without the disruption which is evident in deep dyslexia. These three different dyslexic disorders – surface dyslexia, phonological dyslexia and deep dyslexia – are referred to as **central dyslexias**, since each results from a disruption of the central processes of reading in the brain.

Japanese Dyslexia

Sasanuma (1980) discussed the reading performance of two Japanese patients which bore an interesting relationship to the European patients. One Japanese patient, *Y.H.*, showed superior reading of the kanji symbols which represent whole words (see fig. 7.5). Reading of the kana syllabic representation (see fig. 7.4) was poorer. When the same stimuli were written in one or other of these scripts, there was a superiority of kanji reading over kana reading. Further, the patient made semantic paralexia with kanji: reading, for example, *eye* as 'mouth' and *mountain* as 'forest'. The ability to sound aloud nonsense syllabic strings written in kana, of either two or three characters, was non-existent. So this patient showed poor reading of non-words, made semantic paralexias and found reading of a script, based on meaning, much easier than reading of a script based on syllabic sounds. *Y.H.* resembles cases of deep dyslexia.

In contrast, Sasanuma describes another patient, *K.K.*, in whom the reading of kana was superior to the reading of kanji. The kana reading was nearly perfect and had a 95 per cent accuracy level, whereas in reading kanji only about 50 per cent of the items could be read correctly. This patient would sometimes produce nonsense responses or **neologisms**, which were meaningless syllabic strings. *K.K.* was able to read aloud with accuracy, both two- and three-character nonsense words constructed from kana. In comparing the two patients' abilities to read concrete words and abstract words, *Y.H.* was much better at reading concrete words than abstract words, suggesting a meaning-based reading system, whereas for *K.K.* there was no significant difference between the two groups. *K.K.* is like a surface dyslexic, with preservation of phonological reading mechanisms over those based upon meaning.

The existence of these two contrasting disorders in Japanese, with patterns of reading performance parallel to the reading disorders seen in English, supports the notion that the underlying mechanisms controlling reading performance are similar for the two different languages. Both sets of patients can be explained in relation to a similar underlying reading model, in which the reading of unfamiliar items based upon phonological reading skills is distinct from semantic identification of whole words. Sasanuma's two patients can be explained in relation to a dual-route model of reading.

Direct Dyslexia

More recent theories of reading have suggested that there may be a third reading route which should be incorporated into reading models. The introduction of this third route is based directly on evidence from patients with dementia. As dementia develops there is a gradual deterioration of intellectual skills. Memory is usually affected first and in the latter stages reading deteriorates. In Baltimore, Schwartz, Saffran and Marin (1980) found patients with dementia who were able to read aloud irregular words. Since these cannot be read by a phonological reading route, they must have been read by a semantic reading route. However, when the patients were asked what the words meant, they were unable to provide accurate definitions. They were able to read irregular words for which meaning was unknown. In the dual-route reading model this is not possible, since the patients have apparently accessed the whole word pronunciation without going through the semantic system. So, a third reading route was postulated, which goes directly from the visual-input logogen system, to the store of word pronunciations, bypassing the semantic system (see fig. 7.10). Since this reading route goes directly from input logogens to pronunciations it is called the **direct reading route**.

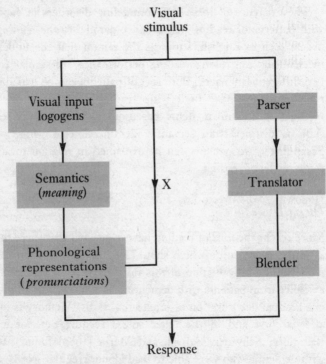

X: The Direct Route

7.10 A triple-route model of reading illustrating the direct route.

Some researchers have argued that different reading routes do not exist and that a single reading route can account for both reading words and reading non-words by analogy with the words.

These **analogy theorists** have only partially developed their ideas and have been less successful in accounting for the range of symptoms seen in the acquired dyslexias.

Recent attempts to model the acquired dyslexias, using parallel-distributed processing models of neural networks, have proved successful in providing an explanation for disorders such as surface dyslexia, which are based upon rule-based systems, but had initial difficulty in accounting for the patterns of performance in phonological dyslexia. In more recent formulations Hinton and Shallice (1990) argue that semantic errors in deep dyslexia can arise within a neural network from phonological impairments but there is not universal acceptance of this proposal.

Learning to Read

Most children learn to speak without explicit instruction, simply following exposure to language in the environment around them and the communicative interactions that they have with family and friends. Reading tends to require explicit instruction. There are occasional cases of children teaching themselves to read, prior to the beginning of formal instruction at school or from parents. More commonly there can be a problem in developing reading, even following conventional instruction. To learn to read competently, a child has to acquire the different reading routes which we have discussed. Traditional models of the development of cognitive skills tend to focus on a sequence of **stages** which are invariant in order, each capitalizing upon the previous stage. These types of models follow the ideas of Piaget (1952) who studied the development of individual children and was particularly interested in the concept of developmental stages. In Piaget's view, at certain critical periods the child acquires specific skills applicable across a whole range of tasks causing a sudden sharp improvement in performance in many areas. A number of Piaget's ideas have been criticized subsequently, and his notion of the universality of these stages is not valid. Children can show competence in understanding certain concepts in one situation when they remain unable to use them appropriately in another situation. Nevertheless, stage theories remain dominant and have been used to describe reading development.

A developmental theory of the acquisition of reading, originally presented by Marsh, has been modified by Frith (1985) who describes a three-phase theory: logographic, alphabetic and orthographic. The phases follow each other in sequential order with each capitalizing upon the previous one. In the first **logographic phase**, a sight vocabulary of instantly recognizable words is built up. Sound-based phonological factors are secondary, so the child only pronounces the word after it is recognized. Then in the **alphabetic phase**, the analytical skill of decoding letters to sounds in sequential order develops. Finally, in the **orthographic phase**, words are systematically analysed into larger units without converting them to sound. These units are internally represented as abstract codes and the codes activate meaning and ultimately pronunciation.

Frith has suggested that the early logographic skills may lead to the establishment of the input logogens of adult models. In contrast, Morton has suggested that these early logographic skills actually use a picture recognition system and that the logogen system does not come into play until the orthographic phase is established later. The alphabetic skills appear to correspond to the development of the phonological reading route. In the logographic stage of reading development, conspicuous letters in words may be important to aid their identification. Letter order tends not to matter, but the child may read a word beginning with a particular letter as another word beginning with the same letter, or may respond to a word with a double *l* in it, with another word with a double *l* in it, for example, *yellow* as 'ball'. In the alphabetic phase, analytical skills develop and letter order becomes very important. The child learns to pronounce new and unfamiliar words. In the orthographic phase, the more sophisticated adult systems of analysis develop. These is some theoretical argument about whether all children progress through these stages in the way in which Frith describes them, but they appear to be an accurate description of the reading development of many children.

Developmental Dyslexia

A significant minority of children fail to develop reading competently despite adequate intelligence and instruction. These children with **developmental dyslexia** provide a problem, both for the educational system and for the families who have to support their children within a system ill-constructed for their needs.

In 1975, the World Federation of Neurology defined developmental dyslexia as being of 'constitutional origin', which implies an underlying biological basis for the condition without specifying its nature. We know that difficulties with reading and spelling often run in families, and that this family history frequently affects boys more than it affects girls. Indeed, in general, boys are more vulnerable to developmental language disorders. It is not yet known whether, in parallel, girls are more vulnerable to developmental disorders of spatial function. There have been several attempts to find a genetic basis for developmental dyslexia. Following linkage analysis (see Chapter One) studies in North America, Smith *et al* (1983) have associated certain forms of developmental dyslexia with a region on chromosome 15. However, in other cases, genetic factors differ. Patterns of transmission do not appear to follow simple Mendelian lines.

Simple brain scans of developmental dyslexics do not show any gross structural abnormality. Nevertheless, there is evidence of some structural difference from the normal pattern. In the majority of right-handed adults an area at the edge of the temporal lobes, called the **planum temporale**, is larger on the left-hand side of the brain than on the right-hand side. This has been postulated as an anatomical substrate for language. In developmental dyslexics there is symmetry of this region across the two sides of the brain (Geschwind and Galaburda, 1985). At first it was thought that this indicated a reduced left planum temporale, but subsequent investigations of developmental dyslexics showed that it was not the left-hand side which was small, but rather it was the right-hand side which was large. New interpretations of these patterns suggest that there may be a disruption of the normal process of cell death in brain development in developmental dyslexia, such that some of the circuitry is not established in the normal way. There are also continuing arguments about whether developmental dyslexics show greater involvement of the right hemisphere of the brain in some of their reading processes, or whether certain sub-groups of them do.

Electrophysiological studies of developmental dyslexia have also been conducted by Duffy and his colleagues (Duffy, Denckla and Sandini, 1980) in Boston. They find differences in the electrical patterns of activity, generated across the skull, in comparison to normal children. There is no single atypical pattern. Some dyslexics show unusual features over the temporal lobes and others show dominant involvement of the frontal areas.

Post-mortem analyses of cases of developmental dyslexia, who have been killed in accidents or by disease which does not directly affect the brain, show surprising results. There are abnormalities of cell migration and areas where the neurons are tangled together (Galaburda, Sherman and Rosen, 1985). The areas of the brain in which these differences are found are relatively broad, extending through a substantial section of the left hemisphere (see fig. 7.11). Such abnormalities are not reported in every patient with developmental dyslexia, but have been found in the majority of the small number studied. The process of post-mortem analysis requires a set of thin slices of brain tissue to be examined in detail. Unfortunately, it is a long and tedious task and it is impractical to imagine that a very large group of brains will be investigated in this way.

Taking together the evidence from the genetic, electrophysio-

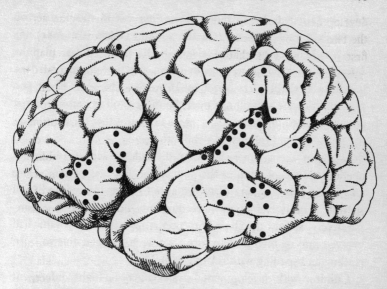

7.11 Topography of ectopias, dysplasias and brain warts in the left hemisphere of a developmental dyslexic studied at post-mortem (Adapted from Galaburda *et al*, 1985).

logical, structural and post-mortem analyses, there is support for the proposal that developmental dyslexia is a disorder of constitutional origin. Despite this, there continues to be substantial ignorance and lack of compassion in the handling of these children in both educational and medical circles.

Children with developmental dyslexia are of normal intelligence, but have specific difficulty in learning to read and to spell. The difficulties that they have are out of line with their other skills. If you meet a dyslexic child they may talk perfectly normally, being able to explain and describe things in an articulate fashion. The difficulty is very specific. It relates to mastery of the written code used in reading.

Estimates of incidence vary, but the population studies done in the seventies by Yule *et al* (1974), in both inner London and the Isle of Wight, suggest that as many as 5 per cent of the population may be affected by this disorder. This would mean that, on average, in each classroom in the country, there is at least one child with developmental dyslexia. Some people argue that the numbers are even more extensive than this. Others feel that the condition is slightly less common. However, whichever figure you take and despite wranglings over the most explicit definition that should be used for diagnosis, there is no doubt that the difficulties are pervasive and frequently debilitating.

It might seem surprising that difficulties with reading and spelling are so common in the population, but it is perhaps more surprising that so many of us are able to learn to read and spell so well. The introduction of reading into our culture is a comparatively recent development, occurring after the brain had evolved into its final human form, yet we have been able to learn reading and spelling with relative ease.

Children with developmental dyslexia may be highly intelligent and some have clear gifts in the artistic, musical, design and engineering fields. Some would make excellent mathematicians and scientists and some good creative artists. Yet for many of these children, unless they are able to attain some measure of formal qualifications in a school situation, it is not possible for them to further develop their education in any formal manner. Thus for some, certain career paths are curtailed. In these cases we, as a culture, lose the benefits of the talents and abilities of the children.

One of the difficulties that there seems to be, in accepting developmental dyslexia as a true disorder with a biological basis, is the difficulty in providing a clear biological correlate in the normal healthy child. Since the doctor and the teacher cannot see the disorder and cannot conduct a simple medical test to illustrate it, there can be a reluctance to accept that it has any reality. A disorder with a basis in the brain may receive unsympathetic management, for the very reason that a direct correlate of brain function cannot be clearly illustrated.

Just as the different reading systems may be selectively damaged following brain injury in an adult who was previously competent at reading and spelling, so they can be differentially affected in development. In developmental surface dyslexia (Temple, 1984) there is selective development of a phonological reading route but impaired development of a lexical reading route. The children read non-words well but have particular difficulty with irregular words, making regularization errors – for example, *yacht* as 'yatched'; *pint* as 'pin-t'. They also show homophone confusion. In developmental phonological dyslexia (Temple and Marshall, 1983) there is selective development of a semantic reading route with impaired development of the phonological reading route. There are significant difficulties in reading non-words and word reading is marked by morphological errors (illustrated earlier in fig. 7.9). In text reading, function-word substitutions are prevalent. Both disorders can be seen in children of the same age and same reading age on standardized tests. Yet the pattern of their problems is strikingly different. This indicates that there is relative independence in the establishment of the different reading routes in development. Developmental phonological dyslexia may be associated with phonological problems on tasks other than reading. These children may also be poor at rhyming and segmenting sequences of speech sounds. Sometimes these dyslexics are referred to as having a language-based difficulty but one should not be misled by this into thinking that their conversational speech will seem unusual. Surface dyslexics do not have comparable phonological problems and perform rhyming tasks and sound-based tasks well.

Developmental deep dyslexia has been an elusive condition. It is rare, though it may sometimes be seen in children with partial hearing loss. The incidence of semantic errors in all the cases reported to date is small, though significantly above chance (Temple, 1988a).

There have been few long-term follow-ups of developmental dyslexia. Phonological dyslexia may persist into adulthood (Temple, 1988b) and in children has been documented consistently in a six-year follow-up. Overall level of performance improves as the years pass but the pattern of the difficulty remains consistent. So, in phonological dyslexia, the number of words which can be recognized by the logogen system increases and the effectiveness of the lexical or semantic reading route increases (see fig. 7.7). However, the difficulty in reading non-words persists and the phonological reading route does not become fully competent. Follow-up of a case of developmental deep dyslexia showed that, following intensive remediation, some minimal phonic skills were finally acquired and semantic errors declined. Amongst acquired dyslexics, there is a report of a deep dyslexic actually recovering so far as to become a phonological dyslexic. Here the deficit in the lexical or semantic reading route has receded.

Spelling

When we are reading, we look at a written code and we work out what words it represents. When spelling, a written code is produced to represent a set of words. In this sense spelling is reading in reverse or is the opposite of reading. However, there are other differences between reading and spelling. In spelling, it is important to know every single letter that has to appear in the words being written. However, in reading it is often possible to recognize a word with partial information about it. We can often recognize a word that is partly obscured, by identifying distinctive characteristics associated with it. It is not always essential to identify each individual letter.

The purposes of reading and spelling also differ. In reading, the objective is to extract the message that is recorded. The objective is to understand. In spelling understanding is not the objective. Spelling involves producing an accurate record. So the tasks have different aims which may affect the underlying systems which control them.

Spelling also has a more sequential character than reading. When we write down words, we write one letter after the other, proceeding from left to right. We do not write a later word in a sentence before an earlier word and we do not write letters at the end of words before letters at the beginning. Although when reading we proceed across the page from left to right, it is possible for us to analyse a whole word in parallel, and within a sentence we may process several words at once. The sequential constraints are not as extreme as in spelling.

When we try to spell a new person's name, or an unfamiliar word, we are often aware of trying to sound out the word as we are working out the letters which should be written down. The pronunciation of the word seems to be used to activate the appropriate letter representations. This suggests that the sound-based codes of spelling – the phonic codes – are accessed prior to activating the correct letters or graphemes. Since we are able to make attempts to spell regular unfamiliar names we know that **phonic mediation** is possible. Also, if you look at the spelling mistakes that people make, they often preserve the overall sound of the word. This is particularly true of spelling errors made by adults and by older children. Phonic mediation is involved, even if it has not produced the perfect answer.

Some spelling performance indicates that there must be another process involved as well as phonic mediation. We must use another system to distinguish between alternative spellings, each of which preserves the sound of a word, but only one of which is correct. We have to know that the correct spelling for 'rain' is *rain*, not *rane* or *raine*. To do this, we must have some **word specific knowledge** about how rain is spelt that tells us which of these possibilities is correct, so there must be information involved which is not sound-based. It is also important to be able to distinguish between different homophones. In order to know whether *sale* or *sail* should be written, you have to know the meaning associated with the word. So, to write some words it is essential to have activated meaning, not just activated the word's sound. Finally, we know that another code is involved in spelling other than phonic mediation, because we are able to spell irregular words. If we were only using phonic mediation, we would spell the word 'yacht' as *yot* or *yott*. Knowledge of how to spell irregular words means that we must have word-specific knowledge, since these words by definition do not conform to spelling rules.

It seems that in spelling, just as in reading, there is more than one way in which we can activate a spelling code. We can use a code that is based on knowledge of the whole word, its meaning and structure, and we can use a code which is based on the sound-based elements of the word. So, in current models of spelling, there are two separate routes for phonological spelling and for semantic spelling. The system which stores knowledge of whole words and knowledge of the sequence of graphemes that must be activated in order to spell them is referred to as the **graphemic word production system**.

Acquired Dysgraphias

Evidence that the two different spelling mechanisms are anatomically distinct comes from studies of brain-injured patients. Patients who have previously been competent in spelling may lose some of these abilities following injury or disease. Two different patterns of spelling difficulty have been described which are relevant to these discussions. Shallice (1981) has described **phonological dysgraphia** in which patient *P.R.* is able to spell over 90 per cent of dictated words, but practically no non-words. This patient is unable to assemble spelling and cannot use the sound-based elements of words to work out their spellings. What he is able to do is to address the spelling of words in the systems that are meaning-based. This pattern of performance is very similar to the dissociation that is seen in reading, in phonological dyslexia. Another spelling disorder, called **surface dysgraphia**, has also been described by Hatfield and Patterson (1983). They describe a patient in whom there is also difficulty with certain elements of spelling. Their patient has problems writing irregular words, which tend to be spelt with a logical rule-based spelling, rather than with the

'gauge' → *gage*	'bury' → *berry*
'laugh' → *laf*	'thorough' → *thurer*
'sign' → *sine*	'flood' → *flud*
'castle' → *casel*	'soul' → *sowl*
'move' → *mouve*	'biscuit' → *bisket*
'gross' → *grose*	'subtle' → *suttle*

7.12 Logical spelling of irregular words by patient *T.P.* (Hatfield and Patterson, 1983).

correct word-specific spelling (see fig. 7.12). The patient, however, is good at spelling non-words and the spelling errors preserve the overall sound of the word. This second pattern of spelling performance is called surface dysgraphia or, by some researchers, lexical dysgraphia or, more confusingly, phonological spelling.

Roeltgen and Heilman (1984) have pointed out that for the eight patients in their study, those with surface dysgraphia had cortical lesions involving the **posterior angular gyrus**, but sparing the **supra marginal gyrus**, whereas those with phonological agraphia had lesions involving the supra marginal gyrus or an area deep within it, but spared the posterior angular gyrus. These different locations are illustrated in fig. 7.13.

Deep dysgraphia has also been described and resembles deep dyslexia in many ways. The patients are unable to write pronounceable non-words. The words they are able to write tend to be high-frequency, highly imageable words. There is no particular difficulty spelling irregular words and most critically they make semantic paragraphias in which the target word and response share meaning, not sound. Examples of such errors are 'time' becoming *clock*; 'sty' becoming *sum*; 'desk' becoming *chair*. They also have difficulty in spelling the short grammatical function words like *our*, *he*, *me* and *you*. Some of these patients appear to have relatively normal reading, so we know that the codes for reading must be

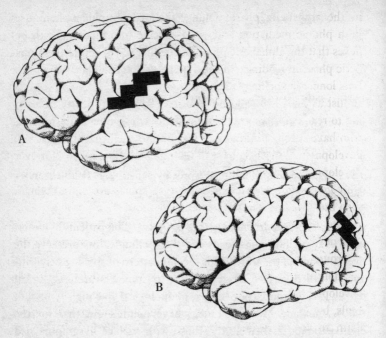

7.13 Areas implicated in dysgraphia: A is the supra marginal gyrus; B is the posterior angular gyrus (after Roeltgen and Heilman, 1984).

separate from the codes for spelling. Cases of deep dysgraphia also show that writing can occur without using phonic mediation, further supporting the notion of two distinct spelling routes.

Spelling Development

Frith's (1985) three-stage model of reading development also discusses spelling development. Spelling is described as going through three phases similar to reading, that is, **logographic**, **alphabetic** and **orthographic**. In the logographic phase the child is able to spell a very small number of words as whole words. Then, sound–based phonic rules of spelling are established in the alphabetic phase; finally, the orthographic system uses both phonic mediation and word-specific information. Frith believes that the alphabetic phase in spelling starts before the alphabetic phase in reading. She also believes that the alphabetic phase lasts longer in spelling.

Just as there are children who have specific difficulty in learning to read, so there are children with developmental dysgraphias who have specific difficulty in learning to spell. All children with developmental dyslexia have developmental dysgraphia. However, developmental dysgraphia can also occur where reading is relatively good. So the developmental dysgraphias are more common than the developmental dyslexias.

The different patterns of spelling development in children with developmental dysgraphia indicate that the phonological spelling route and the word-specific spelling route, whose anatomical locations are distinct in adults, may be differentially affected in development. Some children develop good phonological spelling skills, but fail to master the word-specific information that enables them to spell irregular words and distinguish between homophones. Other children appear to master word-specific information, but have difficulty in mastering the sound-based rules that enable them to produce a logical spelling for an unfamiliar item. The children who failed to master the sound-based rules have a harder time at school, since teachers have difficulty in interpreting their spelling errors, whereas the child who has good sound-based rules may make spelling mistakes which are easily decipherable, since they retain the sound of the word. Those who argue for spelling reforms, in which a logical sound-based code would be used for all words, would make life easier for the children who have learned sound-based rules and have difficulty with word-specific information, but would make life harder for the child who relies upon that word-specific information, since this would become less distinct in modified spelling systems.

Just as there are different types of developmental dyslexia, so there are different types of developmental dysgraphia (Temple,

1986). The pattern of dysgraphia displayed by children of the same age and at the same reading and spelling level on conventional tests need not be identical. In particular, a phonological route to spelling may develop in relative isolation from a lexical semantic route to spelling and vice versa. In the condition where the phonological route to spelling has established relatively well, the label **developmental surface dysgraphia** is sometimes applied. Where the difficulty affects those sound-based rules, but there is good mastery of word-specific knowledge, the label **developmental phonological dysgraphia** is sometimes applied. Some children have impairments of both systems which results in more severe spelling disorders.

For some dyslexic children the pattern of their spelling disorder mirrors the pattern of their reading disorder, so we see surface dyslexia with surface dysgraphia and phonological dyslexia with phonological dysgraphia. However, this need not be the case. There are descriptions of phonological dyslexia occurring with surface dysgraphia. This shows that the sound-based rules involved in reading and spelling are not identical since one may develop in a relatively competent fashion whilst the other is significantly impaired.

Spelling disorders tend to be persistent and will generally still be detectable when children with developmental dysgraphia grow to adulthood. However, both developmental dyslexia and developmental dysgraphia can show significant improvement following focussed remediation. For the adult with a persistent spelling difficulty, word-processing systems with spell-check packages provide a strategy for circumvention.

Chapter Eight :
Emotion and the Brain

Physiological Changes

If you are walking home at night down a dark lane and you hear footsteps behind you getting closer, you may experience a sense of anxiety or fear. This may lead you to change the way in which you are walking. You may walk more quickly, you may begin to run, or you may turn round and look to see who is approaching you. You may feel some degree of tremor associated with this change of pace. You may also experience a sensation of dryness in the throat and may feel your hands beginning to sweat. So, in this potentially threatening situation, you experience an internal sensation of fear and anxiety; you alter the behaviour you are exhibiting; and you also feel certain physiological responses in your body. Your brain is involved in each of these, though you may be aware only of conscious control over the alterations in your behaviour.

Anxiety-provoking situations which are anticipated also have effects. So, if you have to give an after-dinner speech, a speech at a wedding or a talk in front of many people unfamiliar to you, you may also feel some trepidation and anxiety. You may feel a reluctance to begin and may experience the same sweating, dryness of the throat and a feeling of butterflies in your stomach. These sorts of physiological changes are not necessarily associated with unpleasant experiences. In the early days of feeling in love, one may feel anxiety and trepidation about encountering the loved one and these may be associated with paling of the skin or blushing and feelings of butterflies in the stomach. There may also be difficulty in speaking, with voice tremor. Poor motor control may lead to clumsy actions.

The physiological changes in these situations, associated with sweating, alterations in the blood supply to the face and peripheral organs and the internal feeling of butterflies in the stomach, are associated with activities controlled by the **autonomic nervous system** (see fig. 8.1). This is composed of two sections: a **sympathetic system** which evolved to create arousal for situations in which an animal must flee or fight, and the **parasympathetic system** which has a recuperative function, restoring the balance of the body. Thus, heart rate can be increased either by increasing the action of the sympathetic nervous system or decreasing the action of the parasympathetic nervous system. One of the neurotransmitters which is involved in inducing some of these physiological changes is adrenalin and its partner noradrenalin which, in the United States, are referred to as epinephrine and norepinephrine.

The feeling of sweating palms, which we may experience in a situation of stress, is associated with alterations in the activity of the sweat glands, following activation of the autonomic nervous system. This alteration in the sweat on the skin changes the ability of electricity to flow across the skin and, therefore, changes the skin's resistance. This means that if we record the electrical change between two points on the skin, it will vary, dependent on the sweat glands' activity.

Electrodermal Responses

Lie detectors record **electrodermal responses**, a base-line measure of which is taken first. The lie detector is based on the principle that when somebody lies, this causes tension and anxiety which causes an alteration in the activity of the sweat glands, therefore increasing the size of the electrodermal response. A

8.1 The autonomic nervous system.

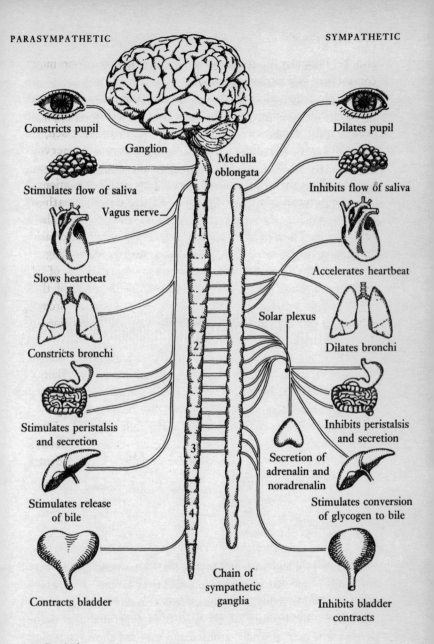

PARASYMPATHETIC   SYMPATHETIC

Constricts pupil   Dilates pupil

Ganglion   Medulla
                    oblongata

Stimulates flow of saliva   Inhibits flow of saliva

Vagus nerve

Slows heartbeat   Accelerates heartbeat

                    Solar plexus

Constricts bronchi   Dilates bronchi

Stimulates peristalsis   Inhibits peristalsis
and secretion   and secretion

                    Secretion of
                    adrenalin and
                    noradrenalin

Stimulates release   Stimulates conversion
of bile   of glycogen to bile

Contracts bladder   Chain of   Inhibits bladder
                     sympathetic   contracts
                     ganglia

1 Cervical
2 Thoracic
3 Lumbar
4 Sacral

number of neutral questions are asked first, each evoking a response. Then the critical question is asked and the magnitude of the electrodermal response is compared with the previous ones (see fig. 8.2). One difficulty with these tests is that electrodermal response can change in any emotional situation. An artificial base-line level of electrodermal response can be created either by thinking anxiety-provoking thoughts or by clenching the toes or fingers when each of the neutral questions is asked. Then there may not be any significant difference between the neutral responses and the lie.

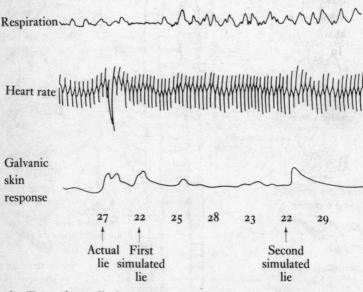

8.2 Traces from a lie detector.

Another problem with the test is that some people have very low levels of arousal in anxiety-provoking situations. If a person is not stressed by lying, then the electrodermal response need not alter unusually because of the lie. It is suggested that some psychopaths may be under-aroused and may not show the typical patterns of responses. Finally, if the subject is aware of which question is critical and is particularly anxious about it even though telling the truth, an elevated electrodermal response to the critical question may occur, thereby giving the appearance of a lie. It is for these reasons that lie detector tests are not considered as admissible evidence in court in the United Kingdom, though in the United States greater significance is attached to their results.

Lie detectors are discussed here as if there is a simple sequence of events. First, a person feels anxious about lying and then they sweat, altering the electrodermal response. However, some early theories considered that the process of sweating itself, and the physiological changes associated with the action of the autonomic nervous system, might contribute directly to the emotional state that was felt.

In the **James–Lange Theory** of emotion (see fig. 8.3), the

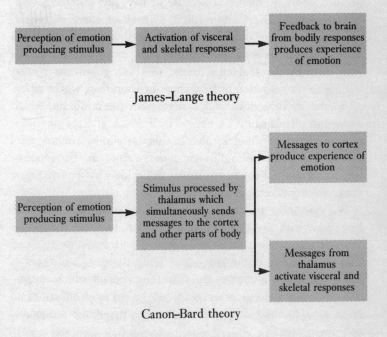

James–Lange theory

Canon–Bard theory

8.3 The James–Lange and Canon–Bard Theories of emotion.

stimulus that is emotion provoking is perceived by the brain, and there are subsequent changes in the sensations that we feel in the body. These are then detected by our senses and the emotion occurs as a result of the observation of these sensations. Thus, the experience of emotion actually results from the perception of the physiological changes. The physiological sensations trigger the emotion. We feel sorry because we cry, angry because we strike and afraid because we tremble. According to this type of theory, if you want to feel happy you should smile and the process of smiling and laughing may in themselves be sufficient to induce the sensation of happiness. Indeed, some psychologists would argue that there is evidence to support this. One difficulty with the James–Lange theory of emotion is that it does not say how we know which emotion to feel. How do we know whether we are shaking and trembling because we are frightened or because we have just won the pools?

According to the **Canon–Bard Theory** of emotion, mental processing and the brain must also contribute to the emotion. When a person faces an emotion-provoking event, nerve impulses pass through the thalamus. Some of these go to the cortex, leading to the sensation of fear, anger or happiness, whilst others go to the hypothalamus and structures in the midbrain, which command physiological changes. The emotion and the physiological reactions are simultaneous. In this way similar arousal states can occur in response to different types of emotion. The processing in the cerebral cortex enables us to decide why we are feeling the physiological changes that we experience.

We can learn to try to change the physiological responses associated with emotion. There is concern that the changes in heart rate and blood pressure associated with response to stress may be damaging in the long-term. Thus, there are a plethora of stress management courses and relaxation courses which encourage professionals and others exposed to stressful situations to learn how to relax and combat the activity of the autonomic nervous system.

Stress Control

Relaxation techniques may also help to combat feelings of panic which may be associated with a particularly threatening or stressful situation. They may reduce the anxiety experienced by some psychiatric patients in situations where intense anxiety is not really justified. In the phobic disorders, excessive anxiety may be caused by a particular stimulus. There may be an unrealistic fear of water (**hydrophobia**), of animals (**zoophobia**), or of spiders (**arachnophobia**). Whilst some of these anxieties need not interfere with everyday life, others are sufficiently intense to inhibit day-to-day activities. In these situations, the phobic may seek clinical help. Intense fear reactions may be particularly problematic if they restrict the movement of the person. **Agoraphobia** is a general fear of open spaces. This can stop the phobic going outside and may be associated with general anxiety about social skills and interacting with other people. **Dromophobia** stops people crossing streets whilst **gephyrophobia** stops them crossing bridges. **Homichlophobia** stops people going out in the fog and **ombrophobia** stops similar excursions in the rain. **Aerophobia** stops travel by plane whilst **siderodromophobia** stops travel by train. Modification and increased control of the activity of the autonomic nervous system is a core component in the management of these emotional disorders.

Brain Structures

In the 1930s, Papez discussed the involvement of structures in the limbic system in the control of emotion. He described a reverberating circuit which was the neural basis of emotion. The geometry of this area is difficult to describe and the anatomical interconnections are complex. In evolution, the limbic system was the earliest form of the forebrain to develop. In primitive animals like the crocodile it is connected with olfaction, leading to either approach behaviour or attack behaviour. In higher animals olfaction is considered to be less important, although there is renewed interest in our responses to pheromones. The midbrain structures in the **circuit of Papez** included the **hypothalamus**, the **thalamic nuclei**, the **cingulate gyrus**, **hippocampus** and their interconnections (see fig. 8.4). Papez said these constituted 'a harmonious mechanism which may elaborate the functions of central emotion, as well as participate in emotional expression.' Papez considered that the organization of his circuit met the physiological requirements proposed by Canon–Bard in their theory of emotion. It was also consistent with previous suggestions that the seat of consciousness was located somewhere near the midline of the brain. This more philosophical issue has induced less subsequent debate than his proposed emotional circuitry.

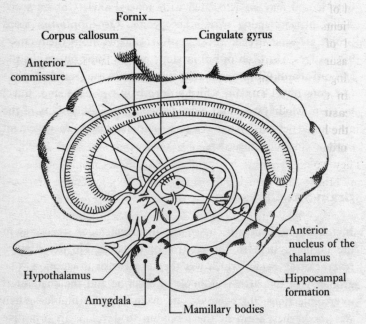

8.4 Interconnections within the circuit of Papez.

Underneath the limbic system, the brain stem contains the **reticular formation**. The reticular formation receives sensory information and acts as a filter, passing on new or inconsistent information. Within the reticular formation is the **locus coeruleus**, or so-called **blue area**, which secretes noradrenalin. Noradrenalin acts on the cortex, the thalamus and the hypothalamus. It also acts downwards on the cerebellum and the spinal cord. The locus coeruleus is, therefore, a concentrated collection of neurons from which there is a divergent circuitry. It has been suggested that noradrenalin may play a role in psychiatric disorder, with too little leading to depression and too much leading to severe stress reactions and neurotic disorders. Noradrenalin may also be associated, however, with feelings of pleasure. Close to the locus caeruleus is the **substantia nigra**, or so-called **black area**, which secretes **dopamine**. Dopamine is involved in the control of movement; disorders in dopamine function are evident in patients with Parkinson's disease, who have difficulty in the control of movements. However, dopamine also facilitates some pleasurable sensations and may mediate exhilaration in people taking certain forms of drugs, such as cocaine and amphetamines.

In the 1950s, Olds and Milner discussed the concept of a **pleasure centre** in the brain. They claimed that this was located in the hypothalamus and pointed out that rats would press a lever in order to gain electrical stimulation to this area of the brain. They would press the lever thousands of times in preference to any other activity, including eating, eventually leading to starvation. This 'reward pathway' follows a similar route to the dopamine-transmitting neurons from the substantia nigra and the noradrenalin-transmitting neurons from the locus coeruleus. Either of these can be activated by electrical stimulation. Some humans have reported pleasurable feelings following electrical stimulation of areas similar to those described as pleasure centres by Olds and adrenalin and dopamine systems may be involved in inducing these sensations.

Gray (1987) has suggested that the **septal-hippocampal**

system, which is a sub-section of the limbic system discussed by Papez, is particularly involved in certain behavioural disorders. Gray observed that when the septal-hippocampal system is damaged the deficits and behaviour seen are similar to those observed after anti-anxiety drugs have been administered. He therefore suggested that the site of action of anti-anxiety drugs is the septal-hippocampal system and, in particular, that anti-anxiety drugs affect the input from **monoaminergic** neurotransmitters.

Gray proposed a model of how the different structures in the limbic system interact. He sees the hippocampus and the circuit of Papez, which links the hippocampal formation to the rest of the brain, as functioning as a comparator 'to monitor ongoing behaviour and the information that comes from the world, so as to check that the former is going according to plan and the latter fits with expectation'. The hippocampus is seen as an interface between emotion and the thinking processes associated with it, that is, the cognition of emotion. It performs functions which can be put at the service of the emotion of anxiety. In other words, when you feel anxious you engage in particular kinds of thought processes which go on in the hippocampus.

Gray suggests that certain clinical disorders can result from abnormalities in the system. If there is excessive anxiety, the checking system is overactive, working too frequently. This may lead to **excessive compulsive neurosis**, a disorder in which patients feel the desire to repeat certain activities again and again, like hand-washing, or have repeated thoughts which they find difficult to drive from their mind. If the checking system detects mismatches too often, then the ongoing systems of behaviour are interrupted too frequently. This may lead to **phobic behaviour**, in which extreme anxiety is produced by certain non-threatening situations.

Emotional Processing

Most of Gray's work and ideas have developed from research with rats. This has led to a debate about the relevance of theories of emotion which are derived from animals so removed from men in the phylogenetic scale. Can human and rat emotions really be compared? In humans there are, for example, cultural influences on perception and vocabulary, which may affect emotion and many other subtleties of behaviour, that are not applicable in the rat. Most people believe that human emotion is not simply the result of monitoring external events but can be influenced by thinking out the emotions themselves. This underlies both the therapeutic relationships with counsellors and psychologists and also the sentiment sometimes expressed that somebody will 'feel better if they talk about it'. For those who prefer to resolve emotional conflicts without interaction with others there is still personal thought about the emotions. People think and reason about why they feel upset and what will make them happy. Do rats do this? Indeed, do rats in their normal day-to-day lives develop obsessive compulsive neurosis or phobic disorders? Despite these arguments, some of the physiological mechanisms described by Gray may underlie components of our own emotional states, with additional complex elaboration, differentiation and interpretation by the cerebral cortex.

We know that the two cerebral hemispheres of the brain have different cognitive capacities. These can lead to asymmetries in behaviour and in the way in which we interpret the world. Many studies suggest that the right hemisphere of the brain is more involved in the perception of emotion and in its expression than the left hemisphere of the brain.

In relation to language, the right hemisphere of the brain is better at interpreting the emotional tone of voice in speech. A typical experiment illustrates this. It uses some sentences with a happy message like 'She won a prize' or 'The sun is shining'. Other sentences are less cheerful: 'He lost all his money gambling' or 'It is raining very heavily', and yet other sentences are neutral with no particular affective content. They are read in different tones of voice, which are either consistent with the sentence's message or in opposition to it. So, although in principle to lose money gambling is unpleasant, if it had happened to a great enemy it might nevertheless induce some sensation of pleasure and it is possible to read the sentence 'He lost all his money gambling' in a cheerful tone of voice. Similarly, some Californians have an unusual enthusiasm for rain and it is possible to read the sentence 'It is cold and rainy' in a cheerful tone of voice. Subjects are asked to categorize the emotional content of the sentence both in terms of the message that is conveyed and also the tone of voice. Two sentences are presented simultaneously, one played to the right ear and one played to the left ear, in a traditional dichotic listening set-up. Since the connections that the left ear makes with the right hemisphere are stronger than the connections the right ear makes with the right hemisphere, any bias towards superior judgements from the left ear is taken as evidence of increased right-hemispheric involvement in the task. In this kind of experiment, the left ear is better at making judgements about the tone of voice, whereas the right ear is better at judging verbal content.

Brain-damaged patients who have sustained injuries to the right hemisphere have difficulty in making such interpretations of affective mood from speech. Their language and communicative systems appear relatively normal, in terms of being able to say roughly what they want to say, but the content of their speech is often emotionally flat, lacking its previous variation and modulation in character and sounding rather dull. In fact, it is suggested that the more creative elements in language are absent. Some of the connotative associations of language may be influenced by the right hemisphere. This may be relevant if the patient was previously involved in professional writing in a creative manner.

The bias of the right hemisphere towards emotional processing can also be shown using visual stimuli. Odd pictorial images of faces can be constructed, which are referred to as **chimeric stimuli**, in which one half of the mouth appears to smile and the other appears to look sad or glum (see fig. 8.5). People are asked

8.5 Chimeric faces.

to rate faces of this sort, whether they look happy or sad. Typically, right-handed people will say that the left-hand face in fig. 8.5 looks happier. They show a bias in favour of judging the emotion of the face on the basis of the emotion that is shown on the left-hand side of the face. This happens even though the person can see that the opposite side of the face has a downturned mouth rather than a smile. The eyes are wired up so that information in the left-hand side of the visual world is initially projected to the right hemisphere, whereas the right visual field projects to the left hemisphere. The bias in judging faces on the basis of their left-hand side as viewed is taken as evidence that the right hemisphere has greater influence in making these emotional judgements.

Some people argue that this bias in chimeric face experiments, or any experiments using face material, actually reflects the superiority of the right hemisphere in face processing. Others have argued that the fundamental characteristic of the right hemisphere, which gives it superiority in face processing, is its capacity to form emotional associations, since faces are, of essence, stimuli which we associate with emotional experiences and emotional situations. Right-hemisphere damage in neurological patients can affect their ability to make judgements about the emotional expression of faces and to make such faces themselves. So these patients have problems identifying the emotional tone of speech, expressing emotionally intoned speech, and also understanding and making emotional facial expressions. The patients have not been studied in great detail, so we do not know whether these problems just tend to cluster together or whether they always co-occur. It would be interesting to know whether there are patients who have greater difficulty in one or other of these tasks; whether the control processes involved in integrating emotion with speech can be differentiated from the control processes involved in conveying emotional facial expressions. The impairment in emotional processing is not specific to either the verbal or the visual modality, nor is it restricted to either the comprehension and understanding of emotion, or the production and generation of it. The deficit is not modality specific.

Emotional Behaviour

Changes in emotional behaviour associated with right- or left-hemisphere disease can also be observed. Right-hemisphere disease can be associated with indifference or even with euphoria. Thus, the patient will often show an astonishing lack of concern about the ailments that may be associated with their condition. Whilst this makes them very easy to work with, it is not, in our terms, an appropriate reaction for them to display. In extreme conditions this indifference to their condition may extend to a complete denial of an ailment. So, a patient with right-hemisphere damage, who has paralysis of the left side of the body, may deny that that side of their body belongs to them. If you ask them why they cannot move their arm well they may say, 'It's not mine, it belongs to Mr Temple in the next bed.'

In contrast, patients with left-hemisphere disease may have depression and may suffer from what has been called 'a catastrophic reaction'. One theory was that this depression might be associated with the common occurrence of language difficulties following left-hemisphere damage. Since this has such a significant impact upon social behaviour and the capacity to communicate with the people around them, it would not be surprising if it caused distress. However, in practice, the depression and negative reactions are not restricted to patients who also have language impairments. The gloom and doom exists independently of any communication problems.

If the right hemisphere of the brain does control emotion, it would not be surprising if emotions showed more conspicuously on the left-hand side of the face, since this side of the face is directly controlled from the right hemisphere. In studies where people are asked to rate the intensity of emotional expressions, taken from films and videos, this is exactly what is found. Most subjects consider that the left-hand side of the face is more emotive. Another way of assessing this is to take photographs of people and section them longitudinally from top to bottom, bisecting the nose. Then pair together two right halves and two left halves, producing two faces which contain absolutely symmetrical halves which have been derived from the same single photograph. When these composite photographs are judged, the ones made from the left halves are judged as having more intense emotions than the ones made from the right halves.

It is said that you can learn about people by watching the way their eyes move. It has been suggested that, when asked a verbal question, people are more likely to look to the right, but if asked a question with emotional content, they are more likely to look towards the left. However, there has been difficulty in the replication of such studies. Certainly we do appear to make involuntary eye movements in a variety of situations, but exactly how these should be interpreted is unclear. What one can sometimes tell from people's eyes is the degree of emotional intensity that they feel. If light levels are kept constant, one of the responses which the autonomic nervous system induces in emotional situations is dilation and constriction of the pupil. In principle, if you want to tell if somebody really likes you, you can look at the size of their pupils and see if they are expanding. However, even if the pupils are constricted, it does not always mean the person dislikes you. For example, intense light also causes pupillary constriction. Knowledge of the responsiveness of the pupils to emotion and our apparent ability to detect it, often without awareness, can lead photographers and advertisers to retouch photographs of people's eyes. They can produce pictures in which the models have larger pupils, which makes them look more appealing to us.

Role of Frontal Lobes

In addition to the hemispheric asymmetries in emotional control and expression, other cortical areas have been emphasized in relation to human emotion. A strong association between the frontal lobes and human emotion has been discussed since descriptions by Harlow, in 1868, of a foreman, Phineas Gage, and his accident at work. Phineas Gage worked for a railroad construction crew. He had a serious injury when a tamping iron was blown into the frontal lobes of his brain. The iron actually entered the skull at one side and exited at the vertex (see fig. 8.6). Amazingly, Phineas Gage did not even lose consciousness; he survived with apparently normal language, memory and perceptual abilities. In an earlier chapter we discussed the association of the frontal lobes with planning and organizational skills; Phineas Gage showed the effects of these deficits by being unable to retain his previous occupation and having difficulty in conducting business and executing plans. The alterations in his emotional state were also striking. Harlow (1868) discusses how the balance between his intellect and his 'animal propensities' had been destroyed. He describes Phineas as being

fitful, irreverent, indulging at times in the grossest profanity, which was not previously his custom, manifesting but little deference for his fellows, impatient of restraint or advice when it conflicts with his

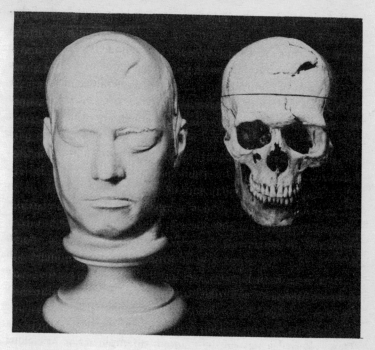

8.6 Mask of Phineas Gage illustrating the damage to the frontal lobes caused by the tamping iron.

desires, at times pertinaciously obstinate, yet capricious and vacillating, devising many plans of future operations, which are no sooner arranged than they are abandoned in turn, for others appearing more feasible.

In humans, the frontal lobes involve almost 40 per cent of the total cortical tissue in the brain. Since this area of the brain has expanded substantially in the evolutionary leap from higher apes to man, studies of animals do not provide full insight into human frontal-lobe activities. Different types of emotional alterations are described in association with frontal disease. In some patients, there are descriptions of apathy and indifference, with a lack of responsiveness to situations and detachment from them. Then there are descriptions of depression and automaticity where the patients are withdrawn and have negative thoughts. It is difficult to induce them to become involved in any activity, other than those which are automatically conducted. These patients are very difficult to work with since they may be very reluctant to initiate any type of activity.

At the other extreme, some frontal patients are restless, exhilarated and euphoric. These frontal patients can be the most enthusiastic research subjects, delighting to participate in anything that is suggested, with an exaggerated degree of excitement and emotion, and showing reluctance to stop participation when the test session comes to an end or the experimenter is exhausted. In such patients there can also be a disinhibited jocularity, where the emotions displayed are not appropriate to the social situation and there is a lack of appreciation of the social context in which they are operating. Some of these patients can act in a way reminiscent of people who are drunken and jocular, that is, they show disinhibited exuberant behaviour which lacks elements of rationality, but which is not necessarily offensive or aggressive. This association may not be random, since one action of alcohol on the brain may be to suppress the normal functional activity of the frontal lobes.

Leucotomies, Drugs and ECT

The association of the frontal lobes with emotional disorders was the justification for the psychosurgical operations which were performed on psychiatric patients over a period spanning at least two decades during this century. In 1935, Egas Moniz attended a meeting in London where Jacobsen and Fulton reported the effects of the removal of the prefrontal area of the cortex on monkeys. In fact, the talk indicated that the operation had a variable effect, but Moniz supposedly stayed only for the first half of the talk, when he heard descriptions of two operations on two animals. Before the operation the animals were highly emotional and subject to violent temper tantrums when frustrated. Afterwards, they appeared indifferent. In the latter part of the talk, Jacobsen and Fulton described a further animal who, following operation, became even more aggressive than it had been previously, but Moniz, by this time, had departed.

Subsequent to this meeting, Moniz persuaded a colleague, Almeida Lima, to operate on the frontal lobes of humans who were having difficulty in controlling emotions or aggression. The enthusiasm for this operation spread so widely that, over a few years, hundreds of **leucotomies** were performed. In 1949, Moniz shared a Nobel prize for this work. However, his life was not all tranquil. He had been forced to retire in 1944, partly because he had become a **hemiplegic**, that is, paralysed down one side, from a bullet which had lodged in his spine. One of his leucotomized patients had shot him.

There were two different methods of operation for these frontal leucotomies, also sometimes referred to as frontal **lobotomies**. In one method, a hole was drilled on each side of the head and a blunt instrument was inserted and rotated in an arc, destroying much of the white matter. In the second transorbital method, a needle was inserted into the brain, by the side of the eye, and rotated. These operations were fairly crude and up to 120 square centimetres of brain tissue would be destroyed.

The rationale for the operation was that the frontal lobes exaggerated the emotional responses of some of the areas in the midbrain and limbic system, whose tracts ascend into the frontal lobes. Cutting off the connections was thought to have a calming effect by reducing the concern which the individual had about the responses being elicited in the midbrain. The operations were carried out on neurotic and obsessive patients, schizophrenics and those with personality disorders. Today they seem crude and unpleasant and it is unclear whether they were of any particular benefit, though some successes were claimed. The rationale behind the surgery may have received more acceptance, in the days before more recent drug developments, for some extremely disabling conditions. For example, in situations of last resort, where obsessive patients are engaging in repeated self-destructive behaviour, some felt there was little alternative but to explore a novel form of therapy. More disturbingly from a political perspective, violent prisoners also received leucotomies and lobotomies and ethical debates have considered the extent of their informed consent.

In these operations, in addition to removal of frontal tissue, the amygdala was also usually removed. The operations had little consistent effectiveness but did have irreversible consequences. In extreme cases there was stupor or death. In many more there was intellectual deterioration. Listlessness, in association with indifference, was not uncommon and seizures were frequently induced.

More recent techniques destroy a much smaller portion of tissue of only a few centimetres. These more restricted operations are claimed to have some effect on certain phobic and obsessive compulsive patients. Unsurprisingly, there are also studies suggesting that patients who have had frontal lobotomies have difficulties in some of the organizational and control processes which have been discussed in association with the frontal lobes in Chapter Two. In addition to the complications of side effects, there is disagreement in relation to the operation itself, regarding the best site to cut or remove. However, some psychiatric patients prefer a leucotomy or lobotomy to the electroconvulsive therapy which is still used extensively and which also has side effects, but again ethical issues arise as to how well the patients understand the implications of the options. Modern psychiatrists generally prefer to alter the neurotransmitter balance in the brains of psychiatric patients by drug treatment, in their attempts at therapy. Such efforts are usually based on theories of the nature of the neurotransmitter imbalance that is generating the condition. However, the level of understanding of these drugs and the neurotransmitter systems with which they interact is at best primitive. The medications undoubtedly alter behaviour and in many cases improve it, but their mode of operation and our scientific understanding of these systems is in the Middle Ages.

Psychiatric Disorders

Major disturbances in affect or emotion are features of several psychiatric disorders. Anxious fear is a central component of the phobias. Feelings of unrealistic elation and joy, with an exaggerated sense of self-worth, accompany mania. Lowered affect, sadness, feelings of worthlessness and guilt accompany depression. Bipolar disorders include rapid transitions from depression to mania. A major disturbance in emotion is also a core component of one of the best-known psychiatric disorders: **schizophrenia**.

Schizophrenia

Marked by a breakdown in the integration of emotions, thoughts and actions, the division between reality and unreality becomes blurred with frequent accompaniment of **delusions** and **hallucinations**. Delusions are beliefs which either distort or have no reality. These may be persecutory delusions, in which the schizophrenic believes that there is a conspiracy against him, including betrayal by friends and the use of bugs and spys. They may also include the attribution of special significance to a trivial event, so that suddenly the movement of a plant, or the angle of a chair, carries meaning. Such delusions may be alarming to friends and family but may also be frightening to the schizophrenic, trapped in a state of isolation.

Hallucinations are distortions of perception, which most frequently consist of hearing voices where there are none. Most of us occasionally have the impression that somebody said something we did not quite hear but when we ask the speaker to repeat it, they claim not to have said anything. In the earlier discussion of speech perception, the ambiguity of continuous speech was discussed. If a tape of speech is dissected and the isolated words are listened to, about half cannot be identified from their physical signals. Yet we hear them with clarity. We hear clear words from a blurred and ambiguous signal. This means that the brain constructs hypotheses about what it is hearing. It is actively processing input, not just passively translating. In schizophrenia, the process malfunctions so that the schizophrenic hears someone talking but there is no sensory input. Significantly, the voices are not usually friendly. They may pass a critical commentary on the schizophrenic's behaviour; they may tell the schizophrenic what to do. They may come from nearby, moving with the schizophrenic, or may emanate from a particular room or waft across the street.

Schizophrenics may report an inconsistency between the emotion expressed and the emotion felt: they cry and look distressed but claim to feel anger. There may be a delusion that the sadness expressed in the tears is being projected on to them from an evil force outside. This is called **passivity**. Frequently, the emotion displayed is inappropriate to the situation. Sudden intense anger may be provoked from a simple offer of a cup of coffee. Laughter and hilarity may follow hearing sad news from a friend. These unpredictable and inexplicable emotional outbursts, in combination with the irrational content of speech, may in turn cause emotional distress to the social contacts of the schizophrenic. As a result there may be a sense of uneasiness and hesitation on subsequently encountering the schizophrenic, which leads to further exacerbation of their own feelings of persecution. At other times, or in other cases, there may be a flattening of emotional response with reduced responsiveness and withdrawal. This may accompany apathy.

There can be a fascinating logic to the disordered thought of schizophrenics. They may be able to explain, step by step, how they have reached their decision or belief. Yet, in this process, there may have been the inclusion of events or details that are not significant, or an interpretation and conclusion are drawn which do not follow accurately from the information given. It is sometimes as if the planning and organizational skills are using the wrong database and the wrong parameters to operate.

Often suffering cyclically with periods of disintegration interspersed with phases of rational lucidity, the schizophrenic may be sensitive, intelligent, perceptive and interesting. It is a common disorder with a lifetime prevalence of nearly 1 per cent. Whilst the lifetime risk of developing schizophrenia is the same for men and women, there is a difference in age of onset. The peak onset for males is between 18 and 25 years. Females have a later and broader peak, from about 26 to 45 years.

Schizophrenia reflects the disordered functioning of the brain and, whilst social circumstances can precipitate the illness, there appears to be a biological basis in the brain and an inherited genetic component which is then vulnerable to environmental events. The risk of developing schizophrenia if there is a first-degree relative with the disorder is 1 in 10. If there is an identical twin who is schizophrenic, the risk is 1 in 2.

Relatively recent studies attempted to locate the region of the 'schizophrenic-predisposing gene' using **linkage analysis** and RFLPs (**restriction fragment length polymorphisms**). Analyses of schizophrenia had focussed on a region in chromosome 5. This followed the description of schizophrenia in a Chinese uncle and nephew who had **trisomy** of a region called 5q11–13, the eleventh to thirteenth bands of the long arm of chromosome 5. This area of the chromosome was present in triplicate rather than the normal duplicate. Sherrington *et al* (1988) studied five Icelandic and two English families using two RFLPs to track the region $5^q11-{}^q13$. They found a strong concordance pattern with a **lod score** of 6.49 meaning that the inheritance pattern of the disease was $10^{6.49}$-fold more likely to have arisen if they were genetically linked than if they were unlinked. However, in the same publication Kennedy *et al* (1988) failed to find linkage to chromosome 5 in a Swedish family and the following year St Clair *et al* (1989) failed to find linkage in a Scottish family. As with linkage claims in several other psychiatric disorders there have now been major retractions of the initially clear-cut statements about gene locus.

Some of the genetic studies suggest that a broader definition of the schizophrenia phenotype may be necessary. The same genetic factors may predispose to schizophrenia and several other psychiatric disorders. Other researchers have emphasized the different subtypes of schizophrenia. Classical descriptions include **paranoid schizophrenia**, the most commonly discussed form; **catatonic schizophrenia**, in which there is rigid immobility; and **hebephrenic schizophrenia**, incorporating uncontrollable laughter. Crow (1980) distinguishes between schizophrenics with positive symptoms, **Type I** (delusions, hallucinations, thought disorder, etcetera), and those with negative features, **Type II** (withdrawal, the absence of speech and social interaction, etcetera). Type I schizophrenics have acute exacerbations, a good intellectual level and good response to antipsychotic medication. Type II schizophrenics have chronic symptoms, intellectual deterioration and poor response to antipsychotic medication. He argues that the brain base of the two disorders differs.

The dominant biochemical theory of schizophrenia has been that it results from an excess of the activity of the neurotransmitter dopamine in the brain. This theory gained popularity in the 1970s when it was also claimed that mania resulted from an excess of noradrenalin or dopamine, and depression resulted from diminished noradrenalin activity.

The evidence supporting the dopaminergic hypothesis of schizophrenia came from several sources. The first related to drug effects. Drugs like amphetamines which increase the activity of dopamine in the brain cause further deterioration in the symptoms of schizophrenics and, in high doses, produce a disorder similar to schizophrenia in previously normal subjects. Antipsychotic medication is effective on this amphetamine-induced psychosis. In cases with a family history of schizophrenia, episodes of amphetamine abuse may be sufficient to tip one over the edge into a permanent psychosis. The dopaminergic system is not the only system stimulated by amphetamines, so the specificity of these effects has been questioned.

The drug L-dopa also increases dopamine activity in the brain.

This treatment is used for patients with Parkinson's disease in which there is a known depletion of the dopamine-producing cells of the **substantia nigra**. In excessive dosage L-dopa also induces schizophrenic symptoms in its users. Meanwhile, the effectiveness of antipsychotic drugs on schizophrenic behaviour is significantly correlated with the affinity of these drugs for dopamine receptors (Creese *et al*, 1976).

Other evidence for the dopaminergic theory comes from analyses of schizophrenic brains themselves. Post-mortems suggest elevated numbers of dopamine receptors in Type I schizophrenics. Elevated levels of dopamine metabolites are also reported. Interpretation of post-mortem data can be complicated by the possible impact of the drug treatments given after the onset of schizophrenia.

Contrary to the dopamine theory of schizophrenia, elevated numbers of dopamine receptors are not found in the post-mortem analyses of Type II schizophrenics (Crow *et al*, 1984). This supports Crow's notion of distinct brain bases for the two disorders. Two studies have looked at dopamine receptor density *in vivo* using PET. Unfortunately, the results were contradictory (Sedrall, 1990).

In the first chapter of this book we discussed the revision of the idea that the brain contained only a small handful of neurotransmitters. We now know that hundreds of neuropeptides act as neurotransmitters and that co-transmitters moderate the activity of other transmitters. With such a cocktail of chemical transmission it is unlikely that schizophrenia could result from a simple excess of one transmitter. Individual differences must also contribute to the cocktail's balance. Female schizophrenics have a much better response to drug treatment than do male.

The dopaminergic theory has been discussed in relation to specific areas of the brain, partly in an attempt to integrate some of the chemical theories with evidence regarding localization of function. Whilst the integration is more speculative than decisive, the localization data has recently been gathering momentum.

The disorganization of schizophrenic thought and action is a central symptom. As discussed in Chapter Two, organizational skills and executive skills are subserved by the frontal lobes of the brain; it is, therefore, unsurprising that schizophrenics are impaired on many tasks of frontal-lobe function (Kolb and Wishaw, 1983). Ingvar and Franzen (1974) have also shown that there is a **hypofrontal** pattern of blood flow in schizophrenia. Recently, Buchsbaum *et al* (1990) combined these ideas and investigated glucose metabolism in schizophrenics carrying out frontal-lobe tasks. Positron emission tomography (PET) scans detected decreased metabolism of ^{18}F-2-deoxyglucose during a vigilance task.

The subject had to watch a continuous series of letters or numbers and press a button every time a particular pre-designated number or letter appeared. Roughly half of schizophrenics perform poorly on this task and they tend to be those with a strong family history of the disorder. Children of schizophrenic mothers who are considered to be at heightened risk for schizophrenia also perform poorly on this continuous vigilance task.

In Buchsbaum's normal subjects there were increases in glucose metabolism in the right frontal and right temporoparietal regions during the vigilance task. Half of the schizophrenics were hypofrontal. So, there is a clear overlap between the areas of the brain activated by the task and the areas of the brain differing between schizophrenics and controls. These results echo findings from the bad old days of psychosurgery of the frontal lobes, when electrical recording from structures deep in the frontal lobes in psychotic patients revealed abnormal frontal EEG in half of them.

Needless to say, the frontal lobes are not the only area of the brain which has been implicated in schizophrenia. On the basis of studies of the galvanic response, Mednick (1970) argued that hippocampal lesions were involved in schizophrenia. Decreased hippocampal volume, gyri, and cell density have subsequently been reported (for example, Jeste and Lohr, 1989), particularly on the left. Reynolds *et al* (1990) report decreased density of GABA uptake sites in the hippocampus and, in the left hemisphere, this decrease correlated with an increased concentration of dopamine in the amygdala. The GABA co-transmitters cholecystokinin (CCK) and somatostatin are also found to be reduced in the hippocampus of Type II schizophrenics.

Hippocampal disorder would be consistent with the memory impairments for verbal material, geometric drawings and faces reported by Kolb and Wishaw (1983). Luchins (1990) argues from animal models that the repetitive behaviours seen in deteriorated schizophrenics, such as hoarding and pacing, may reflect the failure of modulating influences of the hippocampus on dopaminergic tracts.

The temporal lobes lie over the two hippocami and are closely interconnected with them. Gruzelier argues that the neuropsychological performance of schizophrenics indicates left temporal-lobe dysfunction (Gruzelier and Hammond, 1976; Gruzelier, 1986). The hallucinations of schizophrenia could also find a basis in the temporal lobes as they are an infrequently reported concomitant of temporal lobe epilepsy. An increased number of temporal lobe epileptics also report extreme religious conversion following experiences of spiritual visions.

In Chapter Three, the corpus callosum and its possible functional significance in the human brain was discussed. The first case of schizophrenia and callosal agenesis was reported by Lewis *et al* (1988). Subsequently partial callosal agenesis in schizophrenia has been reported in rare cases but at an incidence significantly above the normal expected level. The corpus callosum develops embryologically in close association with the hippocampus and other structures in the limbic system, and in cases of callosal agenesis there may be increased abnormalities in these regions, some of which have also been implicated above in the discussion of schizophrenia. In schizophrenics who do have a corpus callosum, there is evidence of shape distortion in the middle segments (Casanova *et al*, 1990) but this may be secondary to the ventricular enlargement as the corpus callosum lies over the third ventricle. Other studies have suggested that in schizophrenia the corpus callosum is either thicker or thinner than normal. Increased anterior length has also been reported. Some of the inconsistencies and difficulty of interpretation in these latter studies may relate to the limitations of our knowledge about individual differences in the corpus callosum in normal subjects, particularly in relation to sex, handedness, intelligence and age.

With the recent advances in brain-scanning techniques and the improved resolution and detail of the resultant images, there have been increasing numbers of studies measuring the anatomical structure of schizophrenic brains. Several studies suggest that in schizophrenia the ventricular cavities within the brain which contain the cerebral spinal fluid are enlarged. Raz and Raz (1990) have reviewed these studies and find ventriculomegaly in schizophrenia to be a consistent finding. There is some evidence that the degree of enlargement of the third ventricle is greater than the enlargement of the lateral ventricles. Whilst the enlargement is mild in comparison to pathological conditions in which the flow of cerebral spinal fluid is obstructed, it nevertheless corresponds to a 40 per cent non-overlap between the distributions of the schizophrenic and control subjects.

The degree of ventricular enlargement is greater in patients who have been hospitalized for some time. This suggested that it might reflect a progressive degeneration or that it might be a by-product of institutionalization. However, follow-up studies of patients over nearly a decade showed no change in their degree of ventricular enlargement. It seems that patients with more enlarged ventricles may have a more virulent form of the disease and as a result spend more time in hospital. Enlarged ventricular size was also more prominent in samples with a high proportion of men, which is consistent with the greater severity and poorer prognosis of schizophrenia in men.

The lack of change in the degree of ventricular enlargement with age argues against the perception of schizophrenia as a progressive degenerative disease and suggests that there may be a very early prenatal or neonatal abnormality in the brain development of schizophrenics which only expresses itself much later in maturational development (Lewis, 1989). Crow and Done (1986) pointed out that siblings do not develop schizophrenia at the same time in response to environmental stress but they develop schizophrenia at the same age, regardless of the age between them, suggesting the involvement of genetic factors which programme brain development.

Schizophrenia is found in all cultures and has not evolved out of the population. Selection pressures have not been sufficient to eliminate it, suggesting that the predisposing gene may carry positive benefits. The relatives of schizophrenics are variably said to be of high intelligence, higher than usual fertility and to be highly creative. Ultimately, an account of brain function in schizophrenia may have to explain these familial effects as well.

References

Chapter Two

Bernstein, I. L. (1978), Learned taste aversions in children receiving chemotherapy, *Science, 200*, 1302–1303.

Foder, J. (1983), *The Modularity of Mind*. Cambridge, Mass. MIT Press.

Gall, F. J. (1810), *Anatomie et Physiologie du Système Nerveux*. Paris. Schoell.

Luria, A. R. (1973), *The Working Brain*. London. Penguin Books.

Marr, D. (1980), Visual information processing: the structure and creation of visual representations, *Philosophical Transactions of the Royal Society (London), B290*, 199–218.

Penfield, W. and Roberts, L. (1959), *Speech and Brain-Mechanisms*. Princeton. Princeton University Press.

Rolls, E. and Rolls, B. (1982), Brain mechanisms involved in feeding, in Barker, L. (ed.), *The Psychobiology of Human Food Selection*. AVI Publishing Co.

Rozin, P. (1982), Human food selection: the interaction of biology, culture and the individual, in Barker, L. (ed.), *The Psychobiology of Human Food Selection*. AVI Publishing Co.

Schachter, S. and Rodin, J. (1974), *Obese Humans and Rats*. Potomac, Maryland. Erlbaum.

Shallice, T. (1982), Specific impairments of planning, *Philosophical Transactions of the Royal Society (London), B298*, 199–209.

Chapter Three

Dennis, M. (1981), Language in a congenitally acallosal brain, *Brain and Language*, *12*, 33–53.

Ferguson, S., Rayport, M. and Corrie, W. (1988), Neuro-psychiatric observations on behavioural consequences of corpus callosum selection for seizure control, in Reeves, A. G. (ed.), *Epilepsy and the Corpus Callosum*. London. Plenum Press.

Jeeves, M. A. and Temple, C. M. (1987), A Further Study of Language Function in Callosal Agenesis, *Brain and Language*, *32*, 325–335.

Sperry, R. W. (1970), Perception in the absence of the neocortical commissures, in *Perception and Its Disorders*, *Res. Publ. A. R. N. M. D. 48*. New York. Assn. Res. Nerv. Mental Dis.

Temple, C. M. and Ilsley, J. (1993), Sounds and shapes: Language and spatial cognition in callosal agenesis, in Lassonde, M. (ed.), *The Natural Split Brain*. New York. Plenum Press.

Temple, C. M., Jeeves, M. A. and Vilarroya, O. (1989), Ten Pen Men: Rhyming Skills in Two Children with Callosal Agenesis, *Brain and Language*, *37*, 548–564.

Temple, C. M., Jeeves, M. A. and Vilarroya, O. (1990), Reading in Callosal Agenesis, *Brain and Language*, *39*, 235–253.

Vesalius, A. (1543), *De Humani Corporis Fabrica*. Basel.

Zaidel, E. (1978), Lexical organisation in the right hemisphere, in Buser, P. A. and Rouguel-Buser, A. (eds.), *Cerebral Correlates of Conscious Experience*. INSERM. Symposium No 6. Elsevier, Amsterdam. North Holland Biomedical Press.

Chapter Four

Annett, M. (1985), *Left, Right, Hand and Brain: The Right Shift Theory*. London. Erlbaum.

Bastian, H. C. (1898), *A Treatise on Aphasia and Other Speech Defects*. New York. Appleton.

Broca, P. (1861), Remarques sur la siege de la faculté du langage articule, *Bulletin de la Société Anatomique de Paris, 16*, 343–357.

Chomsky, N. (1957), *Syntactic Structures*. The Hague. Mouton Publishers.

Chomsky, N. (1965), *Aspects of the Theory of Syntax*. Cambridge, Mass. MIT Press.

Fromkin, V. A., Krashen, S., Curtiss, S., Rigler, D. and Rigler, M. (1974), The development of language in Genie: A case of language acquisition beyond the "Critical Period", *Brain and Language, 1*, 81–107.

Hart, J., Berndt, R. S. and Caramazza, A. (1985), Category-specific naming deficit following cerebral infarction, *Nature, 316*, 439–440.

Jackson, J. H. (1878), On affections of speech from disease of the brain, *Brain, 1*, 304–33; *2*, 203–222, 323–356.

Jakobson, R. and Halle, M. (1956), Fundamentals of language, *Janua Linguarum, 1*. The Hague. Mouton.

Lichteim, L. (1885), On aphasia, *Brain, 7*, 433–484.

Lisker, L. and Abramson, A. (1970), The voicing dimension: Some experiments in comparative phonetics, *Proceedings of the Sixth International Congress of Phonetic Sciences*. Prague. Academia.

Milner, B. (1974), Hemispheric specialisation: Scope and limits, in Schmitt, F. O. and Worden, F. G., *Neurosciences Third Study Program*. Cambridge, Mass. MIT Press.

Pollack, I. and Pickett, J. M. (1964), Intelligibility of excerpts from fluent speech: Auditory vs. structural context, *Journal of Verbal Learning and Verbal Behaviour, 3*, 79–84.

Warrington, E. K. and Shallice, T. (1984), Category-specific semantic impairments, *Brain, 107*, 829–854.

Wernicke, C. (1874), *Der Aphasische Symtomenkomplex*. Breslau. Cohn and Weigart.

Chapter Five

Baddeley, A. D. and Hitch, G. J. (1974), Working memory, in Bower, G. A. (ed.), *The Psychology of Learning and Motivation*, vol. 8. New York. Academic Press.

Brooks, N. and Baddeley, A. D. (1976), What can amnesic patients learn, *Neuropsychologia*, *14*, 111–122.

Butters, N. (1984), Alcoholic Korsakoff syndrome: An update, *Seminars in Neurology*, *4*, 226–244.

Craik, F. and Lockhart, R. (1972), Levels of processing: A framework for memory research, *Journal of Verbal Learning and Verbal Behaviour*, *11*, 671–684.

De Renzi, E., Faglioni, P. and Villa, P. (1977), Topographical amnesia, *Journal of Neurology, Neurosurgery, and Psychiatry*, *49*, 498–505.

Gardner, H. (1977), *The Shattered Mind: The Person after Brain Damage*. London. Routledge and Kegan Paul.

Hodges, J. R. and Ward, C. D. (1989), Observations during transient global amnesia: A behavioural and neuropsychological study of five cases, *Brain*, *112*, 595–620.

Humphreys, G. and Riddoch, M. J. (1987), The fractionation of visual agnosia, in Humphreys, G. and Riddoch, M. J. (eds.), *Visual Object Processing*. London. Erlbaum.

Milner, B. (1980), Complementary functional specialisation of the human cerebral hemispheres, in Levi-Montalcini, R. (ed.), *Nerve Cells, Transmitters and Behaviour*. Elsevier, Amsterdam. North Holland Biomedical Press.

Milner, B., Corkin, S. and Teuber, H.-L. (1968), Further analysis of the hippocampal amnesia syndrome: 14-year follow-up study of H.M., *Neuropsychologia*, *6*, 215–234.

Parkin, A. J., Blunden, J., Rees, J. and Hunkin, N. (1991), Wernicke–Korsakoff syndrome of non-alcoholic origin, *Brain and Cognition*, *15*, 69–82.

Rabbitt, P. M. A. (1982), Breakdown of control processes in old age, in Birren, J. E. and Schaie, K. W. (eds.), *Handbook of the Psychology of Aging*. New York. Van Nostrand Reinhold.

Scoville, W. B. and Milner, B. (1957), Loss of recent memory after bilateral hippocampal lesions, *Journal of Neurology, Neurosurgery and Psychiatry*, *20*, 11–21.

Squires, L. R. (1982a), The neuropsychology of human memory, *Annual Review of Neuroscience*, *5*, 241–273.

Squires, L. R. (1982b), Comparisons between forms of amnesia: Some deficits are unique to Korsakoff's Syndrome, *Journal of Experimental Psychology: Learning, Memory and Cognition*, *8*, 560–571.

Squires, L. R. and Cohen, N. (1982), Remote memory, retrograde amnesia, and the neuropsychology of memory, in Cermak, L. S. (ed.), *Human Memory and Amnesia*. Hillsdale, NJ. Erlbaum.

Squires, L. R. and Slater, P. C. (1978), Anterograde and retrograde memory impairment in chronic amnesia, *Neuropsychologia*, *16*, 313–322.

Warrington, E. K. and Shallice, T. (1984), Category-specific semantic impairments, *Brain*, *107*, 829–854.

Warrington, E. K. and Weiskrantz, L. (1982), Amnesia: A disconnection syndrome?, *Neuropsychologia*, *20*, 233–248.

Whiteley, A. M. and Warrington, E. K. (1977), Selective impairments of topographical memory: A single case study, *Journal of Neurology, Neurosurgery and Psychiatry*, *41*, 575–578.

Chapter Six

Bodamer, J. (1947), Die Prosop-Agnosie, *Archiv fur Psychiatrie und Nervenkrankheiten*, *179*, 6–53.

Bruyer, R., Laterre, C., Seron, X., Feyereisen, P., Strypstein, E., Peirrard, E. and Rectem, D. (1983), A case of prosopagnosia with some preserved covert remembrance of familiar faces, *Brain and Cognition*, *2*, 257–284.

Davidoff, J. B. (1991), *Cognition Through Color.* Cambridge, Mass. MIT Press.

De Haan, E., Young, A., and Newcombe, F. (1987a), Face recognition without awareness, *Cognitive Neuropsychology, 4,* 385–415.

De Haan, E., Young, A. and Newcombe, F. (1987b), Faces interfere with name classification in a prosopagnosic patient, *Cortex, 23,* 309–316.

Hubel, D. and Wiesel, T. (1962), Receptive fields, binocular interaction and functional architecture in the cat's visual cortex, *Journal of Physiology, 160,* 106–154.

Humphreys, G. W. and Riddoch, M. J. (1987), *To See but not to See: A Case Study of Visual Agnosia.* London. Erlbaum.

Lansdell, H. (1968), Effect and extent of temporal on two lateralised deficits, *Physiology and Behaviour, 3,* 271–273.

Lissauer, H. (1890), Ein fall von seelenblindheit nebst einem beitrage zur theorie derselben, *Archiv fur Psychiatrie und Nervenkrankheiten, 21,* 222–270.

Marr, D. (1980), Visual information processing: the structure and creation of visual representations, *Philosophical Transactions of the Royal Society (London), B290,* 199–218.

McCloud, P., Heywood, C., Driver, J. and Zihl, J. (1989), Selective deficit of visual search in moving displays after extrastriate damage, *Nature, 339,* 466–467.

Ratcliff, G. and Newcombe, F. (1982), Object recognition: Some deductions from the clinical evidence, in Ellis, A. W. (ed.), *Normality and Pathology in Cognitive Functions,* London. Academic Press.

Temple, C. M. (1992), Developmental memory impairment: faces and patterns, in Campbell, R. (ed.), *Mental Lives: Case Studies in Cognition.* Oxford. Blackwell.

Warrington, E. K. (1982), Neuropsychological studies of object recognition, *Philosophical Transactions of the Royal Society (London), B298,* 15–33.

Warrington, E. K. and James, M. (1967), Disorders of visual

perception in patients with localised cerebral lesions, *Neuropsychologia*, *5*, 253–266.

Warrington, E. K. and Taylor, A. M. (1973), The contribution of the right parietal lobe to object recognition, *Cortex*, *9*, 152–164.

Weiskrantz, L. (1986), *Blindsight: A Case Study and its Implications*. Oxford. Oxford University Press.

Zihl, J., von Cramon, D. and Mai, N. (1983), Selective disturbance of movement vision after bilateral brain damage, *Brain*, *106*, 313–340.

Chapter Seven

Coltheart, M. (1980), Deep dyslexia: A right hemisphere hypothesis, in Coltheart, M., Patterson, K. E. and Marshall, J. C. (eds.), *Deep Dyslexia*. London. Routledge and Kegan Paul.

Derouesne, J. and Beauvois, M. F. (1979), Phonological processes in reading: data from alexia, *Journal of Neurology, Neurosurgery and Psychiatry*, *42*, 1125–1132.

Duffy, F. H., Denckla, M. B. and Sandini, G. (1980), Dyslexia: Regional differences in brain electrical activity mapping, *Annals of Neurology*, *7*, 412–420.

Frith, U. (1985), Beneath the surface of developmental dyslexia, in Patterson, K. E., Coltheart, M. and Marshall, J. C. (eds.), *Surface Dyslexia*. Hillsdale, N J. Erlbaum.

Galaburda, A., Sherman, G. and Rosen, G. (1985), Developmental dyslexia: Four consecutive patients with cortical anomalies, *Annals of Neurology*, *18*, 222–233.

Geschwind, N. and Galaburda, A. M. (1985), Cerebral lateralization: Biological mechanisms, associations, and pathology, *Archives of Neurology*, *42*, 428–459, 521–552, 634–654.

Hatfield, F. M. and Patterson, K. (1983), Phonological spelling, *Quarterly Journal of Experimental Psychology*, *35A*, 451–468.

Hinton, G. and Shallice, T. (1990), Lesioning an attractor network: Investigations of acquired dyslexia, *Psychological Review*, 98, 74–95.

Marshall, J. C. and Newcombe, F. (1966), Syntactic and semantic errors in paralexia, *Neuropsychologia*, 4, 169–176.

Marshall, J. C. and Newcombe, F. (1973), Patterns of paralexia: A psycholinguistic approach, *Journal of Psycholinguistic Research*, 2, 175–199.

Morton, J. (1979), Word recognition, in Morton, J. and Marshall, J. C. (eds.), *Psycholinguistic Series*, 2. Cambridge, Mass. MIT Press.

Newcombe, F. and Marshall, J. C. (1980), Transcoding and lexical stabilization in deep dyslexia, in Coltheart, M., Patterson, K. E. and Marshall, J. C. (eds.), *Deep Dyslexia*. London. Routledge and Kegan Paul.

Patterson, K. (1982), The relation between reading and phonological coding: Further neuropsychological observations, in Ellis, A. (ed.), *Normality and Pathology in Cognitive Functions*. London. Academic Press.

Patterson, K., Vargha-Khadem, F. and Polkey, C. E. (1989), Reading with one hemisphere, *Brain*, 112, 39–63.

Petersen, S., Fox, P., Posner, M., Mintun, M. and Raichle, M. (1988), Positron emission: topographic studies of the cortical anatomy of single word processing, *Nature*, 331, 585–588.

Piaget, J. (1952), *The Child's Conception of Number*. New York. Humanities Press.

Roeltgen, D. and Heilman, K. (1984), Lexical agraphia, *Brain*, 107, 811–827.

Sasanuma, S. (1980), Acquired dyslexia in Japanese: Clinical features and underlying mechanisms, in Coltheart, M., Patterson, K. E. and Marshall, J. C. (eds.), *Deep Dyslexia*. London. Routledge and Kegan Paul.

Schwartz, M. F., Saffran, E. M. and Marin, O. S. M. (1980), Fractionating the reading process in dementia: Evidence for word-specific print-to-sound associations, in Coltheart, M.,

Patterson, K. and Marshall, J. C. (eds.), *Deep Dyslexia*. London. Routledge and Kegan Paul.

Shallice, T. (1981), Phonological agraphia and the lexical route in writing, *Brain, 104*, 413–429.

Smith, S. D., Kimberling, W. J., Pennington, B. F. and Lubs, M. A. (1983), Specific reading disability: Identification of an inherited form through linkage analysis, *Science, 219*, 1345–1347.

Taft, M. (1981), Prefix stripping revisited, *Journal of Learning and Verbal Behaviour, 20*, 289–297.

Temple, C. M. (1984), Surface dyslexia in a child with epilepsy, *Neuropsychologia, 22*, 569–576.

Temple, C. M. (1986), Developmental dysgraphias, *Quarterly Journal of Experimental Psychology, 38*, 77–110.

Temple, C. M. (1988a), Red is red but eye is blue: A case study of developmental dyslexia and follow-up report, *Brain and Language, 34*, 13–37.

Temple, C. M. (1988b), Developmental dyslexia and dysgraphia persistence in middle age, *Journal of Communication Disorders, 21*, 189–207.

Temple, C. M. and Marshall, J. C. (1983), A case study of developmental phonological dyslexia, *British Journal of Psychology, 74*, 517–533.

Yule, W., Rutter, M., Berger, M. and Thompson, J. (1974), Over- and under-achievement in reading: Distribution in the general population, *British Journal of Educational Psychology, 44*, 1–12.

Zaidel, E. (1978), Concepts of cerebral dominance in the split-brain, in Buser, P. and Rouguel-Buser, A. (eds.), *Cerebral Correlates of Conscious Experience*. INSERM. Symposium No 6. Elsevier, Amsterdam. North Holland Biomedical Press.

Chapter Eight

Buchsbaum, M. S. *et al* (1990), Glucose metabolic rate in normals and schizophrenics during the continuous performance test assessed by positron emission tomography. *British Journal of Psychiatry*, *156*, 216–227.

Casanova, M. F. *et al* (1990), Shape distortion of the corpus callosum of monozygotic twins discordant for schizophrenia, *Schizophrenia Research*, *3*, 155–156.

Creese, I., Burt, D. R. and Snyder, S. H. (1976), Dopamine receptor binding predicts clinical and pharmacological potencies of antischizophrenic drugs, *Science*, *192*, 481–482.

Crow, T. J. (1980), Molecular pathology of schizophrenia: More than one disease process?, *British Medical Journal*, *2*, 66–88.

Crow, T, J, and Done, D. J. (1986), Age of onset in schizophrenia: a test of the contagion hypothesis, *Psychiatry Research*, *18*, 107–117.

Crow, T. J. *et al* (1984), Catecholamines and schizophrenia: An assessment of the evidence, in Liss, A. R., *Catecholamines: Neuropharmacology and Central System-therapeutic Aspects.*

Gray, J. (1987), *The Psychology of Fear and Stress.* Cambridge. Cambridge University Press.

Gruzelier, J. H. (1986), Theories of lateralised and interhemispheric dysfunction in schizophrenia, in Burrows, N. and Rubinstein (eds.) *Handbook of Studies on Schizophrenia.* North Holland. Elsevier.

Gruzelier, J. H. and Hammond, N. V. (1976), Schizophrenia: A dominant hemisphere temporal-limbic disorder?, *Res. Commun. Psychol. Psychiatry. Behav.*, *1*, 33–72.

Harlow, J. M. (1868), Recovery from the Passage of an Iron Bar through the Head, *Mass. Med. Soc. Publ. 2*, 327–347.

Ingvar, D. and Franzen, G. (1974), Abnormalities of cerebral blood flow distribution in patients with chronic schizophrenia, *Acta. Psychiatr. Scand.*, *50*, 425–462.

Jeste, D. V. and Lohr, J. B. (1989), Hippocampal pathologic findings in schizophrenia: a morphometric study, *Archives of General Psychiatry, 46*, 1019–1924.

Kennedy, J. L. *et al* (1988), Evidence against linkage of schizophrenia to markers on chromosome 5 in a northern Swedish pedigree, *Nature, 336*, 167–170.

Kolb, B. and Wishaw, I. (1983), *Fundamentals of Human Neuropsychology*. New York. Freeman and Co.

Lewis, S. (1989), Congenital risk factors in schizophrenia, *Psychological Medicine, 19*, 5–13.

Lewis, S. W., Reveley, M. A., David, A. S. and Ron, M. A. (1988), Agenesis of the corpus callosum and schizophrenia, *Psychological medicine, 18*, 341–347.

Luchins, D. J. (1990), A possible role of hippocampal dysfunction in schizophrenic symptomatology, *Biological Psychiatry, 28*, 87–91.

Mednick, S. A. (1970), Breakdown in individuals at high risk of schizophrenia: Possible predispositional perinatal factors. *Mental Hygiene, 54*, 50–63.

Olds, J. and Milner, O. (1954), Positive reinforcement produced by electrical stimulation of septal area and other regions of the rat brain, *Journal of Comparative and Physiological Psychology, 47*, 419–427.

Papez, J. W. (1937), A proposed mechanism of emotion, *Archives of Neurology and Psychiatry, 38*, 725–744.

Raz, S. and Raz, N. (1990), Structural brain abnormalities in the major psychoses: A quantitative review of the evidence from computerised imaging, *Psychological Bulletin, 108*, 93–108.

Reynolds, G. P., Czudek, C. and Andrews, H. (1990), Deficit and hemispheric asymmetry of GABA uptake sites in the hippocampus in schizophrenia, *Biological Psychiatry, 17*, 1038–1044.

St. Clair, D. *et al* (1989), No linkage of chromosome $5^q11–^q13$ markers to schizophrenia in Scottish families, *Nature, 339*, 305–309.

Sedrall, G. (1990), PET imagery of dopamine receptors in human basal ganglia: Relevance to mental illness, *Trends in Neuroscience, 13*, 302–308.

Sherrington, R. *et al* (1988), Localisation of a susceptibility locus for schizophrenia on chromosomes, *Nature, 336*, 164–167.

Index

READ MORE IN PENGUIN

In every corner of the world, on every subject under the sun, Penguin represents quality and variety – the very best in publishing today.

For complete information about books available from Penguin – including Puffins, Penguin Classics and Arkana – and how to order them, write to us at the appropriate address below. Please note that for copyright reasons the selection of books varies from country to country.

In the United Kingdom: Please write to *Dept. JC, Penguin Books Ltd, FREEPOST, West Drayton, Middlesex UB7 0BR*

If you have any difficulty in obtaining a title, please send your order with the correct money, plus ten per cent for postage and packaging, to *PO Box No. 11, West Drayton, Middlesex UB7 0BR*

In the United States: Please write to *Penguin USA Inc., 375 Hudson Street, New York, NY 10014*

In Canada: Please write to *Penguin Books Canada Ltd, 10 Alcorn Avenue, Suite 300, Toronto, Ontario M4V 3B2*

In Australia: Please write to *Penguin Books Australia Ltd, 487 Maroondah Highway, Ringwood, Victoria 3134*

In New Zealand: Please write to *Penguin Books (NZ) Ltd,182–190 Wairau Road, Private Bag, Takapuna, Auckland 9*

In India: Please write to *Penguin Books India Pvt Ltd, 706 Eros Apartments, 56 Nehru Place, New Delhi 110 019*

In the Netherlands: Please write to *Penguin Books Netherlands B.V., Keizersgracht 231 NL–1016 DV Amsterdam*

In Germany: Please write to *Penguin Books Deutschland GmbH, Friedrichstrasse 10–12, W–6000 Frankfurt/Main 1*

In Spain: Please write to *Penguin Books S. A., C. San Bernardo 117–6° E–28015 Madrid*

In Italy: Please write to *Penguin Italia s.r.l., Via Felice Casati 20, I–20124 Milano*

In France: Please write to *Penguin France S. A., 17 rue Lejeune, F–31000 Toulouse*

In Japan: Please write to *Penguin Books Japan, Ishikiribashi Building, 2–5–4, Suido, Bunkyo-ku, Tokyo 112*

In Greece: Please write to *Penguin Hellas Ltd, Dimocritou 3, GR–106 71 Athens*

In South Africa: Please write to *Longman Penguin Southern Africa (Pty) Ltd, Private Bag X08, Bertsham 2013*

READ MORE IN PENGUIN

SCIENCE AND MATHEMATICS

QED   Richard Feynman
The Strange Theory of Light and Matter

'Physics Nobelist Feynman simply cannot help being original. In this quirky, fascinating book, he explains to laymen the quantum theory of light – a theory to which he made decisive contributions' – *New Yorker*

Does God Play Dice?   Ian Stewart
The New Mathematics of Chaos

To cope with the truth of a chaotic world, pioneering mathematicians have developed chaos theory. *Does God Play Dice?* makes accessible the basic principles and many practical applications of one of the most extraordinary – and mind-bending – breakthroughs in recent years.

Bully for Brontosaurus   Stephen Jay Gould

'He fossicks through history, here and there picking up a bone, an imprint, a fossil dropping and, from these, tries to reconstruct the past afresh in all its messy ambiguity. It's the droppings that provide the freshness: he's as likely to quote from Mark Twain or Joe DiMaggio as from Lamarck or Lavoisier' – *Guardian*

The Blind Watchmaker   Richard Dawkins

'An enchantingly witty and persuasive neo-Darwinist attack on the anti-evolutionists, pleasurably intelligible to the scientifically illiterate' – Hermione Lee in the *Observer* Books of the Year

The Making of the Atomic Bomb   Richard Rhodes

'Rhodes handles his rich trove of material with the skill of a master novelist ... his portraits of the leading figures are three-dimensional and penetrating ... the sheer momentum of the narrative is breathtaking ... a book to read and to read again' – Walter C. Patterson in the *Guardian*

Asimov's New Guide to Science   Isaac Asimov

A classic work brought up to date – far and away the best one-volume survey of all the physical and biological sciences.

READ MORE IN PENGUIN

SCIENCE AND MATHEMATICS

The Panda's Thumb   Stephen Jay Gould

More reflections on natural history from the author of *Ever Since Darwin*.
'A quirky and provocative exploration of the nature of evolution ...
wonderfully entertaining' – *Sunday Telegraph*

Einstein's Universe   Nigel Calder

'A valuable contribution to the demystification of relativity' – *Nature*. 'A
must' – *Irish Times*. 'Consistently illuminating' – *Evening Standard*

Gödel, Escher, Bach: An Eternal Golden Braid
Douglas F. Hofstadter

'Every few decades an unknown author brings out a book of such depth,
clarity, range, wit, beauty and originality that it is recognized at once as
a major literary event' – Martin Gardner. 'Leaves you feeling you have
had a first-class workout in the best mental gymnasium in town' – *New
Statesman*

The Double Helix   James D. Watson

Watson's vivid and outspoken account of how he and Crick discovered the
structure of DNA (and won themselves a Nobel Prize) – one of the greatest
scientific achievements of the century.

The Quantum World   J. C. Polkinghorne

Quantum mechanics has revolutionized our views about the structure of
the physical world – yet after more than fifty years it remains
controversial. This 'delightful book' (*The Times Educational Supplement*)
succeeds superbly in rendering an important and complex debate both
clear and fascinating.

Mathematical Circus   Martin Gardner

A mind-bending collection of puzzles and paradoxes, games and
diversions from the undisputed master of recreational mathematics.

READ MORE IN PENGUIN

SCIENCE AND MATHEMATICS

The Dying Universe Paul Davies

In this enthralling book the author of *God and the New Physics* tells how, from the instant of its fiery origin in a big bang, the universe has been running down. With clarity and panache Paul Davies introduces the reader to a mind-boggling array of cosmic exotica to help chart the cosmic apocalypse.

The Newtonian Casino Thomas A. Bass

'The story's appeal lies in its romantic obsessions ... Post-hippie computer freaks develop a system to beat the System, and take on Las Vegas to heroic and thrilling effect' – *The Times*

Wonderful Life Stephen Jay Gould

'He weaves together three extraordinary themes – one palaeontological, one human, one theoretical and historical – as he discusses the discovery of the Burgess Shale, with its amazing, wonderfully preserved fossils – a time-capsule of the early Cambrian seas' – *Mail on Sunday*

The New Scientist Guide to Chaos edited by Nina Hall

In this collection of incisive reports, acknowledged experts such as Ian Stewart, Robert May and Benoit Mandelbrot draw on the latest research to explain the roots of chaos in modern mathematics and physics.

Innumeracy John Allen Paulos

'An engaging compilation of anecdotes and observations about those circumstances in which a very simple piece of mathematical insight can save an awful lot of futility' – Ian Stewart in *The Times Educational Supplement*

Fractals Hans Lauwerier

The extraordinary visual beauty of fractal images and their applications in chaos theory have made these endlessly repeating geometric figures widely familiar. This invaluable new book makes clear the basic mathematics of fractals; it will also teach people with computers how to make fractals themselves.

READ MORE IN PENGUIN

PSYCHOLOGY

Introduction to Jung's Psychology Frieda Fordham

'She has delivered a fair and simple account of the main aspects of my psychological work. I am indebted to her for this admirable piece of work' – C. G. Jung in the *Foreword*

Child Care and the Growth of Love John Bowlby

His classic 'summary of evidence of the effects upon children of lack of personal attention ... it presents to administrators, social workers, teachers and doctors a reminder of the significance of the family' – *The Times*

Recollections and Reflections Bruno Bettelheim

'A powerful thread runs through Bettelheim's message: his profound belief in the dignity of man, and the importance of seeing and judging other people from their own point of view' – William Harston in the *Independent*. 'These memoirs of a wise old child, candid, evocative, heart-warming, suggest there is hope yet for humanity' – Ray Porter in the *Evening Standard*

Sanity, Madness and the Family R. D. Laing and A. Esterson

Schizophrenia: fact or fiction? Certainly not fact, according to the authors of this controversial book. Suggesting that some forms of madness may be largely social creations, *Sanity, Madness and the Family* demands to be taken very seriously indeed.

I Am Right You Are Wrong Edward de Bono

In this book Dr Edward de Bono puts forward a direct challenge to what he calls the rock logic of Western thinking. Drawing on our understanding of the brain as a self-organizing information system, Dr de Bono shows that perception is the key to more constructive thinking and the serious creativity of design.

READ MORE IN PENGUIN

PSYCHOLOGY

Psychoanalysis and Feminism   Juliet Mitchell

'Juliet Mitchell has risked accusations of apostasy from her fellow feminists. Her book not only challenges orthodox feminism, however; it defies the conventions of social thought in the English-speaking countries … a brave and important book' – *New York Review of Books*

The Divided Self   R. D. Laing

'A study that makes all other works I have read on schizophrenia seem fragmentary … The author brings, through his vision and perception, that particular touch of genius which causes one to say "Yes, I have always known that, why have I never thought of it before?"' – *Journal of Analytical Psychology*

Po: Beyond Yes and No   Edward de Bono

No is the basic tool of the logic system. *Yes* is the basic tool of the belief system. Edward de Bono offers *Po* as a device for changing our ways of thinking: a method for approaching problems in a new and more creative way.

The Informed Heart   Bruno Bettelheim

Bettelheim draws on his experience in concentration camps to illuminate the dangers inherent in all mass societies in this profound and moving masterpiece.

The Care of the Self   Michel Foucault
The History of Sexuality Vol 3

Foucault examines the transformation of sexual discourse from the Hellenistic to the Roman world in an inquiry which 'bristles with provocative insights into the tangled liaison of sex and self' – *The Times Higher Education Supplement*

Mothering Psychoanalysis   Janet Sayers

'An important book … records the immense contribution to psycho-analysis made by its founding mothers' – Julia Neuberger in the *Sunday Times*

READ MORE IN PENGUIN

A SELECTION OF HEALTH BOOKS

When a Woman's Body Says No to Sex   Linda Valins

Vaginismus – an involuntary spasm of the vaginal muscles that prevents penetration – has been discussed so little that many women who suffer from it don't recognize their condition by its name. Linda Valins's practical and compassionate guide will liberate these women from their fears and sense of isolation and help them find the right form of therapy.

Medicine   The Self-Help Guide
Professor Michael Orme and Dr Susanna Grahame-Jones

A new kind of home doctor – with an entirely new approach. With a unique emphasis on self-management, *Medicine* takes an active approach to drugs, showing how to maximize their benefits, speed up recovery and minimize dosages through self-help and non-drug alternatives.

Defeating Depression   Tony Lake

Counselling, medication, and the support of friends can all provide invaluable help in relieving depression. But if we are to combat it once and for all, we must face up to perhaps painful truths about our past and take the first steps forward that can eventually transform our lives. This lucid and sensitive book shows us how.

Freedom and Choice in Childbirth   Sheila Kitzinger

Undogmatic, honest and compassionate, Sheila Kitzinger's book raises searching questions about the kind of care offered to the pregnant woman – and will help her make decisions and communicate effectively about the kind of birth experience she desires.

Care of the Dying   Richard Lamerton

It is never true that 'nothing more can be done' for the dying. This book shows us how to face death without pain, with humanity, with dignity and in peace.

READ MORE IN PENGUIN

A SELECTION OF HEALTH BOOKS

The Kind Food Guide   Audrey Eyton

Audrey Eyton's all-time bestselling *The F-Plan Diet* turned the nation on to fibre-rich food. Now, as the tide turns against factory farming, she provides the guide destined to bring in a new era of eating.

Baby and Child   Penelope Leach

A beautifully illustrated and comprehensive handbook on the first five years of life. 'It stands head and shoulders above anything else available at the moment' – Mary Kenny in the *Spectator*

Woman's Experience of Sex   Sheila Kitzinger

Fully illustrated with photographs and line drawings, this book explores the riches of women's sexuality at every stage of life. 'A book which any mother could confidently pass on to her daughter – and her partner too' – *Sunday Times*

A Guide to Common Illnesses   Dr Ruth Lever

The complete, up-to-date guide to common complaints and their treatment, from causes and symptoms to cures, explaining both orthodox and complementary approaches.

Living with Alzheimer's Disease and Similar Conditions
Dr Gordon Wilcock

This complete and compassionate self-help guide is designed for families and carers (professional or otherwise) faced with the 'living bereavement' of dementia.

Living with Stress
Cary L. Cooper, Rachel D. Cooper and Lynn H. Eaker

Stress leads to more stress, and the authors of this helpful book show why low levels of stress are desirable and how best we can achieve them in today's world. Looking at those most vulnerable, they demonstrate ways of breaking the vicious circle that can ruin lives.

READ MORE IN PENGUIN

A SELECTION OF HEALTH BOOKS

Living with Asthma and Hay Fever   John Donaldson

For the first time, there are now medicines that can prevent asthma attacks from taking place. Based on up-to-date research, this book shows how the majority of sufferers can beat asthma and hay fever to lead full and active lives.

Anorexia Nervosa   R. L. Palmer

Lucid and sympathetic guidance for those who suffer from this disturbing illness and their families and professional helpers, given with a clarity and compassion that will make anorexia more understandable and consequently less frightening for everyone involved.

Medical Treatments: Benefits and Risks   Peter Parish

The ultimate reference guide to the drug treatments available today – from over-the-counter remedies to drugs given under close medical supervision – for every common disease or complaint from acne to worms.

Pregnancy and Childbirth   Sheila Kitzinger
Revised Edition

A complete and up-to-date guide to physical and emotional preparation for pregnancy – a must for all prospective parents.

Miscarriage   Ann Oakley, Ann McPherson and Helen Roberts

One million women worldwide become pregnant every day. At least half of these pregnancies end in miscarriage or stillbirth. But each miscarriage is the loss of a potential baby, and that loss can be painful to adjust to. Here is sympathetic support and up-to-date information on one of the commonest areas of women's reproductive experience.

The Parents' A-Z   Penelope Leach

For anyone with children of 6 months, 6 years or 16 years, this guide to all the little problems in their health, growth and happiness will prove reassuring and helpful.